Interior Design is <u>Not</u> Decoration and Other Ideas

LAURENCE KING

Stephanie Travis: For Mark, Samantha + Matthew
Catherine Anderson: For Scott + Caroline

First published in Great Britain in 2024 by Laurence King
An imprint of Quercus Editions Ltd
Carmelite House
50 Victoria Embankment
London EC4Y 0DZ

An Hachette UK company

A CIP catalogue record for this book is available from the British Library

Flexiback ISBN 978-1-52943-155-1
EBOOK ISBN 978-1-52943-156-8

Quercus Editions Ltd hereby exclude all liability to the extent permitted
by law for any errors or omissions in this book and for any loss, damage
or expense (whether direct or indirect) suffered by a third party relying
on any information contained in this book.

10 9 8 7 6 5 4 3 2 1

Design: Alexander Boxill
Commissioning Editor: Liz Faber
Cover image: 108, Copenhagen, Denmark, design by
Space Copenhagen (photo: Wichmann + Bendtsen)

Printed and bound in China by C&C Offset Printing Co., Ltd.

MIX
Paper | Supporting
responsible forestry
FSC® C008047

Papers used by Quercus are from well-managed forests and other responsible sources.

Stephanie
Travis

Catherine
Anderson

Interior Design is Not Decoration and Other Ideas

Laurence King

Contents

Foreword

Interior design is <u>not</u> decoration…well, maybe there is some decoration involved, but it is so much more than that. That's why we wrote this book; we want to share the complexities of this innovative, multi-faceted, dynamic discipline. Humans spend the majority of their time inside, and the interior is defined as any space where one lives, works, or inhabits. For this reason, it is important to understand that well-designed interiors have the power to make users feel, engage, and thrive— a successful interior provides the backdrop to a happy, safe, and productive life.

    Interior design is all around us, embedded as it is in our **media + culture**. From the **experience** of an interior to the **conceptual** and **spatial** development of a space, to the many **project types** that interior designers create, there is a lot to consider. As such, we touch on the many aspects of the creative process and include information about the elements that go into an interior, such as the importance of **materiality**, the specification of **products**, and the use of sustainable practices within our **environment**. We also look at the **technical** aspects of an interior and how projects actually get built. We conclude with a look at the **profession**, explaining the studio culture of interior design programs at colleges and universities, the many types of firms and jobs, and the reality that designers continue learning well after their degree. As interior design educators, former practitioners, LEED accredited professionals, and NCIDQ certificate holders, we have decades of experience, insight, and knowledge about the profession… and we want to share them with you.

1.0 ⎯⎯ Media + Culture

Interior design is everywhere…It shapes or defines any space one inhabits, works in, or visits. But if you want to see more than what you can experience in real life, a good place to start is with a **book**. Whether in physical form or an online version, there are countless options, including monographs highlighting a specific designer or firm; books that explore a particular style, such as modern minimalism, bohemian eclectic, or cottage chic; and books that focus on an environment or place, whether country (*Living in Japan*), city (*New York Living*), or coast (*Island Style*). There are also publications that explain the process of design in the form of how-to books, rule books, and handbooks. And don't forget those that examine and elucidate specific aspects of the profession, from macro (elements, principles, ideas) to micro (color, pattern, objects).

The holy grail of books for designers is the so-called "coffee-table book," a term that was first published in 1961 in *Arts Magazine*. These large, beautifully designed volumes displaying stunning photographs and illustrations can be paged through or read, but their attractiveness means that they are often just placed on a table as an accessory. About the time the term was coined, central heating was starting to become more widespread, and furniture was now rearranged around a small central table in the living room instead of the fireplace. This new, functional surface—the coffee table—became a space for beautiful objects that could show off the owners' interests or aspirations. Handsome, overscale visual books increased in popularity, and their frequent emphasis on art, design, or photography was seen as a reflection of their owners' creative culture.

So while you might not be able to afford to live in a chateau designed by Belgian interior designer Axel Vervoordt, you can purchase a comprehensive tome on the subject and prominently display it in your home—expressing your highly refined good taste.

See also History, page 28

Designer   Mark Kiessling
Project   *do you read me?!*
Location   Berlin, Germany

For professionals and aficionados who want to keep up on interior trends, a subscription to a design periodical allows for a monthly or bimonthly flood of inspiration straight to your mailbox—online or otherwise. Each issue will incorporate a wealth of information such as new product lines, design ideas, and methods of implementation; photographs of recent work; and interviews with designers and clients.

Top United States-based magazines include the gold standard for commercial interiors, *Interior Design Magazine*, and the residential leaders *Elle Decor*, *AD* (*Architectural Digest*), and *Dwell*. Britain publishes *Elle Decoration* and *The World of Interiors*, while Australia produces *Vogue Living Australia* and *Artichoke* (the latter featuring commercial and hospitality projects). *Design Anthology* is edited in Australia and Asia, while *Kinfolk*, a slow-living magazine, started in Oregon and now has offices globally. And *Frame*, from Amsterdam, is an edgy pick. These varied visual glossies offer a curated overview of the latest projects from around the globe.

Newspapers, too, cover the topic of interior design, with sections often nestled into larger arts and entertainment sections. These include *Home & Design* in *The Wall Street Journal*; *Architecture & Design* in the *Los Angeles Times*; *Home & Garden* in *The Washington Post*; and in the UK, *The Times Bricks and Mortar* section. These sections explore prominent design ideas and show cutting-edge work, and their presence in credible journalistic news sources emphasizes the importance and interest of the discipline. A separate publication in *The New York Times*, *T: The New York Times Style Magazine*, even has its very own *Design & Interior* section.

This just scratches the surface, as there are a plethora of **periodical and newspaper** options for interested readers of all things related to interior design. What do all these media sources have in common? They highlight originality and provide their readers with ideas—sometimes realistic, other times aspirational—but always inspiring.

See also Books, page 10

Periodical   *Interior Design Magazine*
Issue   Best of Year
Date   January 2021

INTERIOR DESIGN®

JANUARY
2021

BESTofyear

Whether one is young or young at heart, social media plays an enormous role in society to virtually connect people with like-minded others on myriad topics within a wide variety of communities. And this is no different for interior design. Designers share current work with a wide-ranging audience, while users search for designers who match their design aesthetic to get new ideas and advice—it's a win–win.

Unsurprisingly, design lovers flock to visual sites such as Pinterest and Instagram. Once an amateur catches the design bug, they can create and share their own Pinterest board, find designers to follow on Instagram, and search for home design videos on YouTube. Free design apps such as Floorplanner, 3Dream, or Roomstyler are out there for the beginner to explore, enabling them to create a quick plan or virtual model, rearrange and add interior elements, and view the finished work. Those on the educational track—enrolled in an interior design program—will be exposed to more advanced digital tools such as AutoCAD, Revit, and Rhino, which have more sophisticated rendering capabilities. Students can also look to a firm's website for a plethora of information such as its history, philosophy, portfolio, and career postings. LinkedIn is used by professionals to widen their business network, as well as by students and recent graduates on the job hunt.

Navigating **social media and apps** takes patience but, with some refinement, they can open one's eyes to the variety and complexity of the interior design profession. Even while in a Zoom meeting or watching the latest TikTok dance, the interior background can give a lot of information about the speaker or performer. With the exception of text-only-based platforms, interior design has a strong presence on social media, whether it is the main topic or not.

See also Video Games, page 26, and Education, page 210

Designer   Laura Cattano Organizational Design
Project   Private residence
Location   Brooklyn, NY, US

1:33   .ıll 🛜 🔋

‹   Follow

Posts

 laura.cattano   •••

      • • • •

laura.cattano my apartment isn't staged for pictures.
it's staged for how i want to live.

#lauracattano #professionalorganizer #interiorstylist
#smallspaceliving #smallspacedesign

View all comments

If the eyes are the windows to the soul, then **TV** is the window to the world. With what seems like limitless channel choices and a plethora of genres to select from, one could spend endless days and nights just staring into this universe. One category that has strongly emerged on the television platform is interior design. Viewers gain DIY tips and inspiration as they watch designers flip, sell, fix, list, edit, make over, and organize buildings and interiors.

Home tours and real-estate-focused programs give the viewer an unprecedented look at every possible size, style, and type of space. Fictional TV can also influence views: for example, the sitcom *Friends* introduced an eclectic, colorful mix that became known as flea market chic, while the period drama *Downton Abbey* highlighted the jewel tones and florals of the Edwardian style. The series *Mad Men* focused on the advertising world of 1960s New York City and popularized the mid-century modern look using sleek neutrals and classic pieces designed by American designers Florence Knoll and George Nelson. Thanks to TV, these pieces quickly became collectables, yet again.

Just as the small screen has influenced interior design, so has the large screen. In **film**, the interior can become a character as important as a lead actor. *Parasite*, the 2019 South Korean thriller that won an Academy Award for Best Picture, uses the design of the fictional Park family home to infuse the film with a sleek, contemporary style: the set created for the film helps to tell the story. The large, boxy house incorporates a mix of levels; muted, geometric furnishings; and an oversize wall of glass to represent the wealthy Parks, in direct contrast to the dark, cramped semi-basement home of the Kim family. Thus the interiors help viewers understand class and societal differences, while building a visual narrative in connection with the script.

TV and movies will continue to influence interior design...as long as the public keeps watching.

See also Theater, page 18

Image   Jon Hamm as Don Draper in his office
Show   *Mad Men*, Season 7b, Episode 10
Channel   AMC

The lights dim, a hush falls on the audience…and the curtains open. But even before the performance starts, it is the set design that is first noticed by the audience. The creation of an environment on stage sets the tone. Sometimes it is a backdrop, other times the performers interact with it; either way, it enhances the production and storytelling. When the story is set within a specific context, such as an interior, the stage design is critical to establishing the time and place.

New York-based architect David Rockwell has created **theater** sets for many Broadway musicals, including *Hairspray*, *Kinky Boots*, *Catch Me if You Can*, and *Legally Blonde*. He received a Tony Award in 2016 for Best Scenic Design in a Musical for *She Loves Me*. For this set, Rockwell re-created a perfumery in Budapest in the 1930s: the shop exterior opens like an overscale dollhouse, revealing an Art Nouveau-style retail fantasy complete with spiral staircase and mezzanine. The comedy *Plaza Suite* by Neil Simon incorporates three short plays, all taking place in a single suite in New York's famed Plaza Hotel in the late 1960s. The set of the show's 2022 Broadway revival, by set designer John Lee Beatty, reflects an old-money luxury suite with traditional faux-French touches such as upholstered furniture, mix-matched wood antiques, decorative lighting, heavy drapes, and extensive paneling. Sets such as these not only bring the story to life and stimulate the audience but also expose interior design to audiences of varied backgrounds.

One can't go back in time to 1930s Budapest or 1960s New York, but the theater can immerse the viewer in the interior design of different eras through the stage design experience.

See also Lighting, page 146

Designer   David Rockwell

Project   *Legally Blonde: The Musical*

Exhibits inform and educate the viewer in a visual, compelling way. A topic such as interior design—which everyone is surrounded by but many don't think critically about—is both interesting and relevant for an exhibit. It can be experienced on many levels: the macro level (the design of the museum, gallery, or other public space), the meso level (the design of the exhibit itself), and the micro level (the content of the exhibit). What other topic can carry through from the content to the design to the interior where the exhibit is located?

The Museum of Modern Art (MoMA) in New York exhibited *How Should We Live? Propositions for the Modern Interior* (2016–17), which displayed spaces through the lens of society, including politics, technology, and culture from the 1920s to the 1950s. Further uptown at the Metropolitan Museum of Art, a re-creation of a living room from a 1914 house by American architect and interior designer Frank Lloyd Wright allows one to experience his core concept of horizontality through elements such as low, blocky furniture, geometric lighting, and linear ornament. Exhibits such as these introduce the importance of interior design in history, and as a worthwhile discipline of study within the arts.

Search past exhibits at any major design museum and there will be a range of topics that incorporate interior design, such as *Germany Home Stories: 100 Years, 20 Visionary Interiors* (2020-21) at the Vitra Design Museum in Weil am Rhein, Germany, and the Triennale di Milano's *Home Sweet Home* (2023), which explored the home through a contemporary lens. From London (Design Museum) to Singapore (Red Dot Design Museum), Denmark (Designmuseum) to Israel (Design Museum Holon), museums with a design focus are present in cities around the globe, waiting to be explored.

See also Circulation, page 82, and Cultural, page 106

Project   *How Should We Live?*
             Propositions for the Modern Interior
Location   MoMA, New York, NY, US

Of the 36 surviving oil paintings by Dutch master Johannes Vermeer, nearly all incorporate the domestic interior, providing a view into the hidden world of women in their 17th-century domain. And, while his paintings depict light in the most beautiful manner, his unrivalled portrayal of architectural details such as decorative window panes, checkerboard flooring, carved wood furniture, and everyday accessories allows the viewer to experience the interiors of that time through **art**.

Fast-forward to the 20th century and Henri Matisse's *The Red Studio* transports the viewer into his studio outside of Paris around 1911, while David Hockney's *Large Interior, Los Angeles* from 1988 approaches the artist's own home in a cubist manner—a geometric mix of floor, wall, and ceiling, detailed with brightly colored patterns and furniture. A few years later, American pop artist Roy Lichtenstein used the Ben Day dot process (in which multiple small, colored dots are combined to produce different areas of color) to create the works of his *Interiors* series (1990–91), inspired by advertising and consumerism, which give a basic modern interior a jolt of irony. A contemporary artist who portrays the interior in her work is Los Angeles-based, Nigerian-born Njideka Akunyili Crosby: her collages incorporate minimalist architectural detailing, oversize terrazzo flooring, sleek furnishings, and highly patterned surface coverings that include meaningful imagery that speaks to social and political issues, an example being the work *Dwell: Aso Ebi* (2017).

The representation of interiors is also seen in three-dimensional art, as in the work of contemporary German artist Henrike Naumann. Her installations incorporate residential furniture and accessories, in tandem with audio and video, to create narratives using the seemingly simple domestic interior to make a statement.

As is evident, the interior has been portrayed in art throughout history in varied and thoughtful ways: it's a lot more than just a backdrop.

See also Cultural, page 106

Artist   Roy Lichtenstein
Work   *Interior with African Mask* (1991)
Collection   The Eli and Edythe L. Broad Collection

It can be difficult to determine exactly which design discipline is influencing another, as there has always been a push and pull between creative fields. And sometimes there is an outright overlap of stylistic approaches, as evidenced by the **fashion** and interior design icon Marie Antoinette, the Austrian-born French queen of the late 18th century. With her love of elaborate haute couture in luxurious fabrics, she fit right in with her interiors, which were decorated with matching floral textiles, pastel boiserie (symmetrical carved-wood detailing incorporating lavish flowers, leaves, and urns), and furniture covered with motifs from classical architecture. Her holistic approach to fashion and interiors continues to impact current designers. Consider her the world's first influencer.

Interior design continues to play a role in fashion, as evidenced by more recent collections, such as the influence of British interior designer David Hicks on American sportswear designer Tory Burch, who pored over Hicks's archives from the 1960s to create her spring/summer 2018 collection that exudes his spirit. Bold, symmetrical patterns in textiles and rugs such as those used in *Hicks' Hexagon* and *Octagon*, which consist of interlocking hexagons and octagons respectively, in striking color combinations, were eventually interpreted into a wearable assemblage.

Arabesque interior detailing, with its intricate curvilinear forms, symmetrical patterns, and architectural pointed arches with scalloped edges, influenced the spring/summer 2016 collection designed by Clare Waight Keller, then creative director of French fashion house Chloé. And Louis Vuitton, inspired by French designer Charlotte Perriand's colorful furniture and methods of prefabrication, created its spring/summer 2014 collection with reversible, removable, and expandable clothing as well as accessories that stress utility, function, and beauty.

It was British fashion designer Mary Quant, icon of London mod fashion of the 1960s, who famously said, "Fashion is not frivolous. It is a part of being alive today." Second that for interior design.

See also Inspiration, page 58

Designer   Clare Waight Keller for Chloé
Project   SS2016 Collection

The Court of the Myrtles
(detail), The Alhambra,
Granada, Spain

Video games have come a long way since *Pong*, the 1972 digital table-tennis game by Atari, where users moved a paddle up and down the side of a box on the screen to keep the ball in play. With augmented and virtual reality, games have exploded to include hyperrealistic settings and interaction. It's no surprise that computer software from the gaming industry is overlapping into the interior design field, and vice versa. Some interior designers are even putting their talents to work for giants such as Microsoft, Epic Games, and Blizzard, creating realistic and fantastical interiors for a variety of action and activity games. It is common for interior designers to use programs such as Revit to produce three-dimensional renderings for design projects; and now, combined with software such as Unreal Engine, these creations can become the backdrop for a real-time video adventure.

Popular games such as *Fortnite* and *Minecraft* have allowed millions of players to create their own designs for the interiors and buildings of a three-dimensional world in which they compete and explore a variety of challenges. *Minecraft*, where players use blocks to generate their structures, conjures up the textile-block houses designed by the American architect Frank Lloyd Wright in the 1920s, where he used molded concrete to create solid and geometric-patterned blocks.

For those less interested in the adventure and more in the design aspect, there are plenty of video games that focus on the creativity of interiors. With games such as *Home Design 3D*, *Design My Room*, and *Design Home: Home Renovation*, players can design the room or home of their dreams, take on daily challenges, share design ideas, and be a part of a community of other inspiring designers. In *Design Home*, players can incorporate virtual products and furniture from real brands into their designs, and then order the actual product for their real home. Now, that's life imitating design imitating life.

See also Social Media + Apps, page 14

Designer   Mojang Studios
Project   *Minecraft* lobby

Throughout **history**—from Mesopotamia to the modern day—interior design reflects the social, economic, political, and physical context of place. With the evolution of styles and movements—Gothic, rococo, neoclassical, and postmodern, to name just a few—the history of interior design is both diverse and complex. Although it overlaps with architecture, it has an independent place in the history books, as seen in *History of Interior Design* by Jeannie Ireland, first published in 2008, which is a comprehensive (600-page!) text that explores interiors throughout time.

The history of the interior design profession itself has a more recent timeline. The term "interior decorator" was used in the early 1900s to describe upper-class women with a penchant for furnishing and embellishing homes. A good eye prevailed, since no education was required or available. One such arbiter, New Yorker Elsie de Wolfe, considered the first interior decorator, authored a book titled *The House in Good Taste* in 1913, which is still in print today. Another New Yorker, Dorothy Draper, quickly followed in 1923 with the first legitimate interior design business, which turned out high-profile projects such as hotels, designed in her maximalist style.

American interior designer Florence Knoll—educated in architecture, and one half of the furniture company Knoll Industries—further legitimized the profession with her designs for the corporate workplace, as seen in the Columbia Broadcasting System (CBS) offices completed in New York in 1964. An expert on space planning, she utilized partitions with bold, primary blocks of color; elegant modern furnishings of her own design; and sculptural pieces commissioned from renowned designers. Her dedication to detail, organization, and design elevated the profession.

See also Research, page 54

Designer   Florence Knoll
Project   The President's Office
               CBS, Madison Avenue
               New York, NY, US

2.0 ___ Experiential

The golden section (or golden ratio) is a mathematical ratio that has been known since antiquity; it is closely related to the Fibonacci sequence, in which each number is the sum of the two preceding numbers (0, 1, 1, 2, 3, 5, 8…). As well as fascinating mathematicians, the golden section has been applied as a way of visually measuring or defining beauty in both natural and man-made structures. But isn't beauty in the eye of the beholder? Not necessarily so. The golden ratio generates proportions that are seen as particularly harmonious and aesthetically pleasing when applied in art, architecture, and design. The Fibonacci sequence can be expressed in a tiling of squares whose side lengths are successive Fibonacci numbers, creating the effect of squares that continue to rotate into ever larger squares, all with the same proportion. A spiral can be created by drawing arcs connecting the corners of the squares: this spiral approximates to the golden spiral, itself based on the golden ratio. The golden ratio can also be found in nature—for example, in the spiral patterns of certain seashells and flowers.

The Fibonacci sequence was first discussed by Indian poet and mathematician Acharya Pingala around 200 BCE, although it was named after Italian mathematician Leonardo of Pisa (known as Fibonacci), who described it in his famous book *Liber Abaci* in 1202. The golden section, recognized by the Greeks as embodying **harmony**, beauty, and perfection, is evident in the proportions of many ancient Greek buildings, including the Parthenon in Athens.

The 1st-century BCE Roman architect Vitruvius wrote a pivotal book titled *De architectura*, which explored the ideas of *firmitas*, *utilitas*, and *venustas*—or strength, utility, and beauty—concepts that are still considered when designing functional, harmonious spaces.

Designers consider the psychology of proportion and how it makes people feel in order to create balance in their work. This does not mean a space has to be static or symmetrical to create stability; on the contrary, asymmetrical, dynamic spaces can still have strength. Interior designers are skilled in the art of balancing elements and thereby achieving harmony, epitomized when a space comes together and just…works.

See also Scale, page 90

Designer   Bates Masi + Architects
Project   Private residence
Location   East Hampton, NY, US

The science that measures the physical features of a person is known as **anthropometrics**, which includes all the dimensions and ratios of the human form such as height, weight, body mass, and head and body circumference. Renaissance artist and scientist Leonardo da Vinci famously drew his *Vitruvian Man* (*c.* 1490) to represent his concept of the ideal proportions of the human figure. Swiss-French architect Le Corbusier updated the idea in the 1950s with a more modern take with his Modulor Man: this was based on his Modulor system, which again brought anthropometrics into the picture, centering as it did on the idealized human form as a basis of measurement.

Depending on the task one is designing for—fixed postures or active, moving positions—anthropometric measurements are available. Used in medical fields as well as in a variety of design disciplines such as fashion, industrial, and interiors, such measurements are crucial to creating products and spaces that meet the needs of people, and not the other way around.

French designer Charlotte Perriand created the interiors for much of Le Corbusier's work, including his Unité d'Habitation (residential complex) La Cité Radieuse in Marseille, France, in 1952. Now a UNESCO World Heritage Site, this project was a new, affordable housing model consisting of apartments and communal spaces. Le Corbusier stated that "the kitchen in Marseille should become the center of French family life," which Perriand expressed exquisitely through a colorful, abstract design that allowed for a view across the apartment. Using anthropometrics and aspects of Le Corbusier's Modulor, her compact, highly functional kitchen incorporated a cost-saving standardized design, industrial materials, and forward-thinking elements such as an integrated sink waste disposal and accessible icebox. Ultimately, Perriand designed a space that efficiently and elegantly fit all the needs of the user. As she declared, "The extension of the art of dwelling is the art of living." In other words, she gave life to Le Corbusier's buildings.

See also Accessibility, page 194

Designer   Bestor Architecture
Project   Bestor Architecture Office
Location   Los Angeles, CA, US

Using anthropometric data, designers create functional spaces and products, which is referred to as **ergonomics**. This term comes from two Greek words, *ergon* (to work) and *nomos* (natural law), and was first used in a series of articles by Polish scientist Wojciech Jastrzębowski in the 1850s. However, it was British psychologist Hywel Murrell who popularized the application of ergonomics and is credited for getting the term into the English dictionary in the 1950s. Soon after, ergonomic organizations were created in the United States and Britain, emphasizing the importance of implementing data in the design of things that people use or inhabit. Also referred to as human factors, this data was first used by the US military for tools and machinery, but is now a key component in interior design— specifically in high-traffic spaces, such as commercial kitchens or assembly lines, which require routine tasks.

With the advent and greater usage of the computer, the workplace has become a key focus in the application of the power of ergonomics. According to the US Department of Labor's Occupational Safety and Health Administration, workplace injuries cost companies billions of dollars. Poorly designed workstations decrease productivity and increase the possibility of serious conditions—for example, carpal tunnel syndrome, a common work injury caused by repetitive movement such as improper or prolonged use of a keyboard, touchpad, or mouse.

A standard workspace is more complex than meets the eye; requirements that need to be considered include a comfortable and adjustable task chair to facilitate strong posture for long periods of time, a table and monitor at the appropriate height and distance from the user, the correct positioning of the keyboard, and the type of mouse used. Multiply these considerations for the design of a large workplace, with hundreds of workers, and interior designers need to factor various aspects of ergonomics into their plans for many different work activities, from individual workstations to large conference rooms.

See also Mind + Body, page 178

Designer   Bestor Architecture
Project   Nasty Gal HQ
Location   Los Angeles, CA, US

The theory of **proxemics** is used as a guide within the early phases of a project, specifically in the space planning and layout. Developed by the American anthropologist Edward T. Hall in the late 1950s and early 1960s, it considers the amount of space deemed comfortable between a person and others for different activities. This distance can vary from person to person based on their experiences and personality, but strong similarities are found among people of the same culture. These behavioral traits are measured across four defined spaces—intimate, personal, social, and public—as each define a range of acceptable distances.

In the United States, preferred spaces between individuals are: up to 18 inches (46 centimeters) for intimate or informal conversations, such as chatting with close friends; 18 inches to four feet (46–120 centimeters) for semi-formal interactions, such as talking to a colleague or business associate; four to 12 feet (1.2–3.6 meters) for more formal communication, such as in a classroom with a teacher or professor; and 25 feet (7.6 meters) for larger, more public spaces, such as a lecture or event. In 2020, the term "social distancing" was added to the dictionary, referring to the six-foot (two-meter) distance that people should maintain during a contagious outbreak, in this case COVID-19.

An interesting exploration conducted in the 1960s by Canadian psychologist Sidney Jourard was the "coffee study." He studied nonverbal communication between people in coffee shops in cities in four different countries to determine how often they touched one another, and concluded that certain cultures communicated readily via touch, while others kept to their intimate bubble. Such ideas and studies are intriguing and something to consider, but there is no one-size-fits-all formula; therefore, interior designers use this kind of information as a baseline, but look to the specific activity and user group to expand on known proxemics.

See also Anthropometrics, page 34

Designer   Clive Wilkinson Architects
Project   Stanford Redwood City Campus
Location   Redwood City, CA, US

In his painting series *Homage to the Square*, German-born American artist
Josef Albers explored the complexity of color relationships. Each of these
hundreds of paintings consists of three or four squares, nested within one
another, some of which he presented in his pivotal book, *Interaction of
Color*, written in 1963. A *Dictionary of Color Combinations*, based on the
pioneering six-volume work of Japanese artist and color theorist Sanzo Wada
in the 1930s, reveals traditional Japanese perceptions of color, with 350
combinations per volume. These key works are a part of **color theory**—simply
defined as the means that designers use to determine what colors to use.

     The colors we see daily that we describe with a word such as "red"
are just one small part of the complexity that is color. This is the hue—in paint,
a pure pigment; or in light, a color's defining "dominant wavelength." But
saturation, or how pure it is—i.e. how much gray is in it—and the brightness,
or how light or dark it is—i.e. how much white is in it—are equally important
to designers. This can be seen in the color wheel, invented in 1666 by
English physicist Isaac Newton. He studied the way in which light passing
through a prism splits into a spectrum of colors—what we call a rainbow
when we see it in the sky—and he wrapped this into a circle. This famous
infographic, developed, explored, and refined over the centuries,
communicates the information in a simple manner.

     Color exploration typically starts with the primary colors (red, yellow,
blue) followed by secondary colors, which are created when the primary
colors are mixed (for example, red and blue make purple). Mix secondary
colors to get tertiary colors, and so on. Complementary, or opposing, colors
on the wheel work well together, as do analogous colors, which are grouped
next to one another. Rooms painted in warmer, darker colors will appear
smaller, tighter, and hotter than the same room painted in a lighter, cooler
color, which will appear larger, more expansive, and colder in temperature.
Colors also look different depending on artificial lighting, natural daylighting
during different times of day, and even against other colors.

See also Color Psychology, page 42

Understanding the **psychology of color** is yet another tool in the palette selection process for an interior designer. It's no surprise that different colors can make users feel a certain way. Although there are differences between regions and cultures, we can say that broadly, blue conveys positivity, yellow optimism, red enthusiasm, and green serenity. The most common "favorite" color across the globe is blue—the color of the clear, vast ocean and the sky—which is not surprising as humans crave the calming colors of nature. By contrast, look at the branding of fast-food restaurants, and notice that red pops out as the dominant color in logos and store design, followed by orange and yellow—fiery colors that are considered to stimulate the appetite.

White is often used in interior design as a neutral background: for example, the "white-box art gallery" puts the emphasis on the artwork, not the interior space. From a scientific lens, white and black portray the absence of color; when mixed together, black and white produce a range of grays from the white to the black end of the scale, known as "grayscale." When white is added to a color, it is known as a "tint"; when black is added to a color, it is known as a "shade." Additionally, the term "monochrome" refers to a color scheme using a single color in many tones, while "ombre" (French for shadow) indicates when a color transitions from light to dark or when one color fades into another. Designers acknowledge the emotional connection between humans and color, and use these techniques to make users *feel*: for example, an all-beige, monochromatic interior might evoke calm while a bright, ombre interior might precipitate excitement.

In 2014, Iranian-French designer India Mahdavi, dubbed the "queen of color," had three months to create the Gallery at Sketch in London. Her color scheme, consisting of pink on pink on pink, was an instant favorite on Instagram. The space was so popular that when Mahdavi redesigned it in 2022 using a lemony monochrome, style experts declared millennial pink "over" and yellow the new "it" color.

See also Color Theory, page 40

Designer   Sasha Bikoff Interior Design
Project   Otherland
Location   New York, NY, US

Why is symmetry in design so pleasing? Perhaps because humans visually connect with a space that exudes a sense of balance and order. In other words, what one sees is what one gets (twice). **Patterns** are created by repetition—sometimes geometric, other times organic, but always a line or shape that repeats in a predictable fashion, sometimes having been mirrored or rotated. When viewing a pattern, the whole is greater than the sum of its parts.

Gestalt theory (from a German word meaning "form," or, loosely, "pattern") was developed by three German psychologists in the early 20th century. They approached patterns from a broader viewpoint, with findings that indicate the human mind tends to perceive patterns in its visual surroundings. Among the six common principles of gestalt theory are symmetry (similar, though unconnected, symmetrical elements are perceived as a coherent shape or whole), similarity (elements that look similar are perceptually grouped together), and proximity (elements that are close together are perceived as part of a group). The human tendency for pattern making goes back even further, to our earliest days: when trying to survive in a world of danger, pattern making allowed the species to read disorder. It's also why humans prefer smaller patterns to larger ones, as it was easier to spot a threat.

Along with natural and abstract patterns (think meanders, waves, spirals, bubbles), humans have invented patterns in the decorative arts for centuries, if not millennia—examples from around the globe including *block* from Africa, *ikat* from Indonesia, *damask* from Italy, *tartan* from Scotland, *herringbone* from Egypt, and *toile de Jouy* from France. In an interior, patterns in products such as textiles, wallcoverings, tile, and stone can make an impact, as they connect to the context, enforce the concept, create visual interest, and add depth and meaning to a space.

See also Wallcoverings, page 158

Designer   Neri&Hu
Project   The Muted Landscape
Location   Shanghai, China

Let the sunshine in! All good spaces are connected to an exterior, but just how much external factors play into the interior is up to the designer.

Designers who maximize **natural light** inside bring a sense of warmth and happiness to an interior. According to the US Environmental Protection Agency (EPA), people spend around 90 percent of their time indoors, meaning that our exposure to sunlight is minimal. Seasonal affective disorder—referred to by the apt acronym SAD—was first identified in 1984 by Dr. Normal Rosenthal at the National Institute of Mental Health, describing the "winter blues" that occur in certain people at the time of the year when there is least sunlight. Conversely, sunlight itself has proven to be a mood booster.

The association between sunlight and health is not a new phenomenon: Greek physician Hippocrates ordered sun baths in 400 BCE to cure his patients' ailments; British nurse Florence Nightingale founded modern nursing in the mid-19th century partially on the premise that the sick need direct sunlight to recover more quickly; and Finnish architect Alvar Aalto designed his famous Paimio Sanitorium in 1932 for tuberculosis patients from the inside out—to reflect the sun's path. A recent exploration is Dr. Richard Hobday's book *The Light Revolution: Health, Architecture and the Sun*, published in 2006, which delves into the idea of natural sunlight as a significant health benefit in interiors.

Ultimately, designers determine how to bring the most sun into a space by studying factors such as the orientation of the building and the paths the sun takes through the course of a day in relation to the interior spaces. Plants need sunlight to live, and so do humans.

See also Daylight, page 174

Designer   Clive Wilkinson Architects
Project   Microsoft Pebble Beach
Location   Redmond, WA, US

While it might seem odd that the design of the inside is so closely linked to the outside, there is no denying that humans crave nature. The term **biophilia** is a combination of two ancient Greek words, *bios* (life) and *philia* (love). This "love of life" tendency was named by German-born American psychologist Erich Fromm, who used the phrase in 1964 to describe "the psychological orientation of being attracted to all that is alive and vital." The concept was popularized by the book *Biophilia*, written in 1984 by American biologist and professor Edward O. Wilson, who used the word to characterize "a deep and natural affinity between the human mind and the natural world."

Designers incorporate biophilia into their work in varied ways, which include the creative use of natural light within all interior spaces, including core spaces that lack windows; strategically aligning views toward exterior windows or installing photography or other artwork that expresses nature; specifying indoor planting, such as a green "living" wall, or using well-designed artificial plants; and incorporating water elements through reflecting pools and fountains. The look of water can also be simulated through materiality (such as fluted glass) or by playing audio tracks with the sound of soothing rainfall or a bubbling brook. These are all elements that provide a peaceful connection to the outside environment.

Materials such as rugged flagstone, grained wood, and textured wool also bring a sense of authenticity to an interior. No additional decoration is needed when a wall made from onyx has a beautiful vein pattern, as seen in the interior of the iconic Barcelona Pavilion in Barcelona, Spain, completed in 1929 by German- American architect Ludwig Mies van der Rohe, with interiors by German interior designer Lilly Reich.

See also Connection to Nature, page 176

Designer   Clodagh Design
Project   Alchemy Bar Workshop
Location   Kaplankaya Resort, Bozbük, Turkey

Although interior design is a visual discipline, designers incorporate more than just sight. Sound, smell, and touch are three more senses that must be addressed through **sensory balance**. An awareness of the approximate "sound level"—defined as the noise of the users, including all background noise, that an activity will reach in a given space—is balanced with auditory comfort through the selection of interior construction and material finishes. Acoustic panels can be integrated into walls and ceilings, while a greater use of soft materials throughout a space (such as upholstered banquettes in a busy restaurant) will absorb more sound. Hard materials typically reverberate or bounce sound off their surfaces: therefore designers use products that will combat echoes and noise such as acoustic glass (with a sound-blocking membrane laminated between two pieces of glass) and various sealants.

Along with sound, smell can have a profound effect on the user's experience of a space. Odors can vary and can also be subjective, as many tie in with human emotion and play on memory. Spaces that incorporate scents, such as retail or hospitality premises, often use new aromas; with no prior association, these can create new memories. Other project types use established sensory connections to evoke past memories. Aside from intentional aromas, good interior air quality and circulation is essential to dissipate odors and maintain pleasant smells.

Touch is another powerful sense that is awakened in design, since an interior is meant to be used by people who interact with its materials daily. The feel of a natural material such as wood or stone is different from that of a man-made material such as glass, steel, or plastic. Different textiles, whether natural or synthetic, will also stimulate different responses: a wool rug feels soft and luxurious underfoot, while a sisal mat feels coarse and textured, and a nylon throw will feel different again. For the interior designer, it all needs to make "sense."

See also Comfort, page 180

3.0 ⸻ Conceptual

The general public's perception of the creative process is often that it is triggered by a single flash of inspiration, frequently referred to as intuition. In fact, Japanese architect Tadao Ando states that "design requires one to simultaneously consider and digest an endless variety of matters, in order to make decisions based on a number of relationships. What transcends these concerns is intuition." That first impulse may be the point of departure, but the practice always returns to understanding and integrating the parameters, constraints, or potential problems that are always a part of the design process. This is where **research** is vital: it is an integral part of the design solution or the impetus for the design concept. Often it is the history of the location or building that is the point of inspiration for a project.

Examining precedents or case studies is a way of developing a better understanding of a project type or any facet of a process, such as programmatic, spatial, or conceptual development. Looking at other buildings and spaces to see how others have addressed similar design questions provides a framework to begin.

Research can also be framed within the lens of advancing the knowledge base of the discipline. Academics, but also a few practitioners, will write peer-reviewed articles or books: such contributions expand upon the body of knowledge that defines and renews the discipline. Some firms devote resources to understanding particular aspects of their clients or project types, such as healthcare. This kind of research, applicable for practitioners, can create "best practices" to follow. Most often, however, the designer's investigation is local—recognizing a particular aspect of the building code that needs to be applied or being aware of the limitations of a specific material before it's specified—and these investigations must be considered prior to solidifying the design and presenting to the client.

See also Context, page 56, and Process Part I, page 220

Design Student   Mary Armintrout
Project   Studio work

All interior projects, of any scale or type, are by definition located within a "shell," or a building (which can also be referred to as architecture). This pre-existing condition eliminates the ability for interior designers to select a site; however, the **context** or place can certainly influence the concept or design approach. Christian Norberg-Schulz, author of *The Phenomenon of Place*, writes that "when man dwells, he is simultaneously located in space and exposed to a certain environmental character…to gain an existential foothold man has to be able to orientate himself; he has to know where he is. But he also has to identify himself with the environment, that is, he has to know how he is in a certain place." The building's past use or its historical style, as well as the neighborhood, city, or country, can heavily influence the design of its interior spaces. Design in an urban context might incorporate the rigid grid of a city as a way of organizing spaces, or in a rural site might mimic a minimalist view with long, continuous horizontal planes.

Interior designers also incorporate global and cross-cultural perspectives of the project location when developing design concepts. If the interior reflects a "place," it allows for creative opportunities that would not occur otherwise. Take the brand Aesop—a skin, hair, body, and home line with a strong visual identity—and its approach to designing retail interiors to connect to the site's location. With more than 200 retail shops in countries from Singapore to South Korea and the United States to the United Arab Emirates, the company uses the design of each store to reflect its location with a unique point of view. Why should they all be the same? Interior designers, by employing context to create robust conceptual ideas, produce compelling designs that connect projects to specific locations.

See also History, page 28, and Research, page 54

Design Student   Magenta Livengood
Project   Studio work

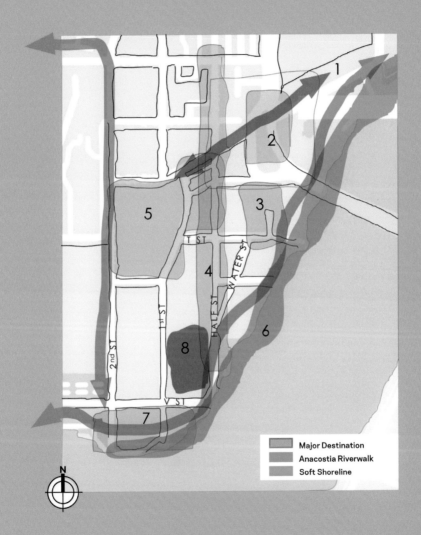

Canadian designer Bruce Mau states in his *Incomplete Manifesto for Growth:* "Work the metaphor. Every object has the capacity to stand for something other than what is apparent. Work on what it stands for." Mau's insight informs, noting that one need not travel far to find **inspiration**: it can truly spring from anywhere and anything. Designers must be aware and curious, and think divergently. It is about paying attention to the exterior world and keeping a notebook handy to jot down observations, as well as examining one's own experiences or inner thoughts. To have a treasure trove of ideas, one must replenish the mental shelves with ideas; staring at a blank page only reinforces the problem when the mind is fresh out of inspiration. Stocking the empty cupboard happens most frequently when one gets outside and sees the world—with eyes that observe and look as if for the first time. Sometimes this is difficult, since looking at the same place, visiting the daily coffee shop, taking the same way to and from work, does not provide novelty. The unfamiliar alleviates boredom and removes assumptions, replacing them with curiosity and freshness; this is one of the main reasons why traveling, for many, provides a deep treasure trove of inspiration.

Insight may strike quickly and unexpectedly. If the designer can harness this, it is all well and good—but making it visible, working through its development to bring it to fruition, is where it transitions from an idea to reality. There are many sources of inspiration but the hard work of bringing something into existence from a mental image is in the hands of the designer.

See also Process I, page 220

Pragmatically, a project must meet criteria established by the client, safety codes, and any other objectives initiated by stakeholders. But what is the difference between an interior that merely functions well and a space that delights the senses? Most often, the latter was designed with a concept or overarching idea in mind, whereas the former tends to be nondescript and not very memorable. Another way to define the concept is the "**big idea**," or "parti," an architectural term from the French *parti pris*, meaning "decision taken."

These concepts can be drawn from any source of inspiration; the challenge lies in adhering to the idea consistently but without predictability, making it visible but with some restraint. An example of how an idea can give life to a project is a students' adaptive reuse project for a retail space in a historic cardboard factory using the concept of folding forms, a nod to the building's history. In this project, the students designed a material change in the floor, which emerged into a three-dimensional element that folded on itself throughout the space, serving as a shelving system to display products, then as the cashier station, and finally as product storage. All the decision making, from textiles with a fold pattern to the design of the product packaging, was based on a single concept.

Another way to consider the implementation of a concept is writing. To begin, one must have an idea of what to express. It could also be thought of as a thesis statement. Deviating from the idea creates an incoherent paper that is extremely difficult to follow, leading to misunderstandings. In the same manner, a concept can guide the design process and help the designer to make decisions about what or, more importantly, why something should be done. This can be especially helpful when explaining the design to the client and convincing them of the merit of the choices that were made.

See also Inspiration, page 58, and Ideating: Writing, page 62

Design Student Danielle Lee
Project Studio work

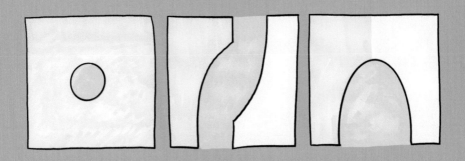

Generating ideas can be a challenging task—where or how does one begin? Interior designers use the following **writing** exercises: spontaneous and unedited word associations, analysis of synonyms or antonyms, and elaborating on a design-vocabulary word and the images it generates. These strategies can be influential during the first phase of the design process.

Writing also helps to organize thoughts, as the initial jumble of ideas can cloud the mind and obscure a path forward: documentation creates a physical representation of the elusive design process. Writing is a basic and simple step that designers use to translate creative thoughts to reality, as words enable one to convey images and feelings to self, colleagues, and clients. Writing frees up the mind as it gets something on paper, very quickly, before the thought slips away. Being able to see one's thoughts on paper later allows for incubation and affords the ability to go back and edit.

Writing and designing are not dissimilar activities, as the "big idea" acts as a sort of thesis for a paper. The first draft of a book is certainly not ready for publication, just as the first strokes of the pencil on paper cannot be built. Writers and designers work iteratively, meaning that both activities require going back, again and again, refining, editing, deleting, redoing. Even looking at particular words, for example verbs, can help designers to think about space and the manipulation of forms—take a look at *Verb List,* a word-based artwork by the American abstract sculptor Richard Serra from 1967, and one can see how it might have been possible for the words to translate to three-dimensional form once he started writing them down.

See also Big Idea, page 60

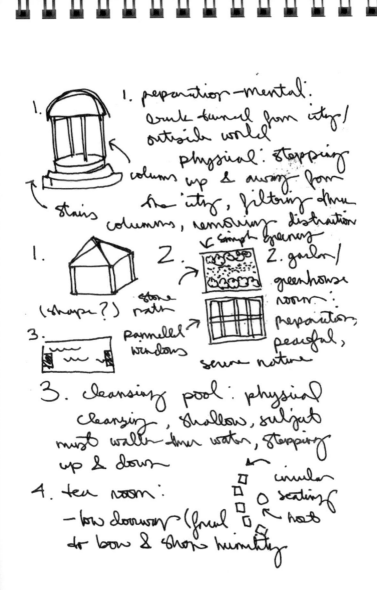

1. 1. preparation — mental:
route tunnel from city/
outside world
physical: stepping
columns up & away from
the city, filtering thru
columns, removing distraction

1. (shape?)   stone path   2.   2. garden/
greenhouse
room:
preparation,
peaceful,
serene nature

3. pannelled windows

3. cleansing pool: physical
cleansing, shallow, subject
must walk thru water, stepping
up & down

4. tea room:
— low doorway (forced
to bow & short humility

circular
seating
host

To draw is to think visually, to make one's ideas visible in two-dimensional form. American architect Steven Holl is known for carrying a small pad of watercolor paper with him and documenting the sensation he experiences on-site. The resulting paintings are not necessarily a precise recording or testament of what he sees but, rather, his thoughts and emotions aroused by the location.

Sketching and drawing act as a universal language that can transcend culture and time. Long before the written word was conceived, the cave paintings in Lascaux, France, represented something significant to the artists and all who viewed them at the time. After thousands of years, they continue to awaken our imagination. And while we are unable to fully comprehend what the painters were trying to convey, the images are recognizable; the viewer can make a connection with the artists by "seeing" how they interpreted their world. The author of the drawing enables ideas to come to life; they are no longer thoughts but possibilities, potential realities. Designers also work through complex ideas or relationships through diagrams and graphic drawings that communicate, clarify, and distill information into discrete chunks that do not overwhelm.

This loose, analog approach opens a wide range of possibilities for the designer, in contrast to the computer-generated document, which gives the perception of completion or finality. Because of this, the initial phase or stage of design greatly benefits from the sketch, which allows iterations, rather than the rigidity and specificity of digital drawings. What the computer affords—rapid duplication and accuracy—is what inhibits the quick and spontaneous ideas that are critical during the initial stages of idea generation.

There is a humanity and warmth to freehand drawings as well as a spontaneity that springs forth from the mind to the hand: this kind of thinking is made visible through sketches.

See also Drawings, page 92

Design Student   Magenta Livengood
Project   Studio work

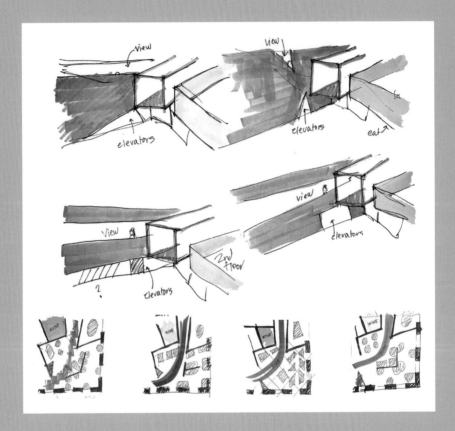

Daily life goes on in rooms within buildings, but these areas need not be relegated to walls meeting at 90-degree angles with nondescript overhead planes. Architects aren't the only ones to give life to forms—interior designers do as well. Yet the architect's design generally relates to the exterior context and, while there are constraints that restrict a structure's form, it is a different process from that of creating interior spaces. A designer's work parameters are contained within the confines of the building's envelope and, most often, the space between the floor slabs. What can be produced is limited only by these constraints and by the imagination. Round, organic contours; sharp, angular configurations; cozy, small enclosures—these are some ways that interior spaces can be expressed. Such forms generate a wide variety of experiences and feelings, which support an overarching concept as intended by the designer.

Through the use of color, materials, patterns, and textures, designers furnish an additional layer of articulation, presenting a sense of scale, beauty, and harmony; however, before this can occur, forms determine the literal framework for the finishes. Together with the arrangement or organization of these volumes or shapes, circulation— how one moves through space in a coherent manner—must also be considered, along with the functional needs of the users.

The most straightforward method of **form making** is to create three-dimensional models. These miniature-scale replicas of a space provide a tangible translation of an idea, enabling both creator and client to sense what it might feel like inside that space.

See also Geometries, page 84, and Three-dimensional Models, page 94

Design Student   Ryan Fowkes
Project   Studio work

Any designer engaged in the act of creating is continually thinking. But the creative, practical, and strategic procedures that designers typically use in **design thinking** offer a creative way of approaching and solving real-world problems, and the methodology has been adopted by other industries and professions.

It may appear self-evident, but design is never executed for its own sake: the user—a human—must always be considered when approaching any kind of problem. Viewing an issue from another person's perspective can prompt care or empathy, thus inspiring the drive to improve living or working conditions through design. Fulfilling people's needs through this intention is the approach that a professional or student in a design-oriented discipline must consider, as well as the behavior and psychology of how all humans react to sensory input within spaces.

The next step involves defining the problem, followed by ideating—through writing and sketching—to generate and explore a range of solutions. An important part of the process is working iteratively. Designing anything requires a method of constantly fabricating while simultaneously unraveling the work, in an effort to hone it and bring the project closer to the envisioned goals. Prototyping, or producing a preliminary representation through software-generated perspectives, can provide visuals to elicit feedback and critique. Refinement is required afterward, perhaps then calling for retreat to generate more ideas. This back-and-forth is not a linear process; at times, it may seem that progress has stalled; however, a certain amount of experimentation and reversal is necessary for this process to flourish.

Designing may not become easier over time, but cultivating trust in this way of knowing, making, and doing brings one closer to an appreciation of the seemingly contradictory ways to approach design.

See also Ideating: Writing, page 62, and Ideating: Sketching, page 64

Design Student   Soorin Chung
Project   Studio work

In many professions, there is a language that must be mastered; discernment of nuances and use of shorthand terms are developed over the years in any industry. This is true of interior design: to convey intent or describe a project comprehensively and concisely, one must first understand **design vocabulary** so that its language is spoken correctly. Providing critique requires the awareness and recognition of terms that have the same meaning for all designers, regardless of location and time: there is a universality to it. For example, when the word "hierarchy" is used, many call to mind a pyramid-shaped diagram with the most important element at the upper vertex, or an organizational chart with a few "important" people at the top and others ranked on the lower levels. In this manner, hierarchy is shown to mean the minority few above the majority below. The same word when used in the context of design vocabulary is used to refer to the way elements are organized in a design so as to emphasize the relative importance of all the elements in a space: this can be expressed through size, color differentiation, or a particularity such as a unique shape.

Francis D. K. Ching, in his book *Architecture: Form, Space, and Order*, notes that "the principle of hierarchy implies that in most if not all architectural compositions, real differences exist among their forms and spaces…For a form of space to be articulated as being important or significant…it must be made uniquely visible. This visual emphasis can be achieved by endowing a form or shape with exceptional size, a unique shape, or a strategic location."

Being able to describe spaces, elements and ideas with appropriate vocabulary is just as important as the ability to execute a project using those same words, as it provides specificity to the interior designer's intention and is at the basis of effective communication.

See also Ideating: Writing, page 62

Design student   Bryce Delaney
Project   Studio work

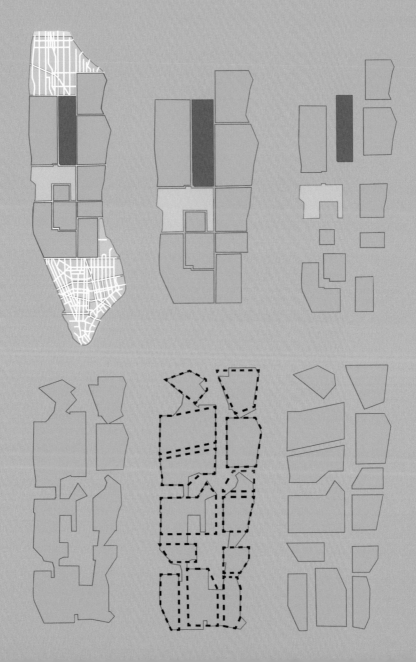

Creating anything requires a discerning eye and unflinching honesty—from both oneself and others—to improve the idea, advance it to a new stage, and bring it closer to a resolution. A **critique**, or an act of judging, starts with one's education in the discipline, where a student and the studio professor have a series of desk critiques (or "crits") to review the progress of the project. These times together are valuable, since this assessment of the work and interaction are conducted in "real time," or in the moment, requiring the instructor and student to have a back-and-forth discussion about how the project is developing and what other design strategies should be considered. This requires the student to present ideas as something visible—be it sketches, study models, writings, or images. Critiques, however, aren't reserved just for students and professors—professionals receive feedback from their peers and certainly from the client.

By some, it is perceived that the goal of the critique is merely to survive an onslaught of harsh words and negativity. But it is to be hoped that the delivery of the message is not insensitive, and the objective is to accept the feedback about the work as shown and use it to improve the work. Design is never completely done or definitively resolved until the project is due (it is often time, money, or both, that forces designers to put their pencils down); because of this, the process must be iterative.

Being simultaneously editor and creator can be difficult; someone with fresh eyes, who has distance from the design and a different way of thinking, is needed. Being open to this kind of dissection can be intimidating and, as a result, critiques often generate apprehension. But when conducted with trusted colleagues and/or studio professors, not only can a critique transform a design but, ultimately, one's design acumen begins to mature and the ability to critique truly begins.

See also Studio Culture, page 208, and Education, page 210

4.0 ⎯⎯ Spatial

Programming refers to the initial phase of a project before the design is executed. This critical stage solidifies the understanding of the client's needs and desires. What spaces have been identified? Is there anticipation of growth? Are there any areas that must be adjacent? What are the functions or processes that require particular attention or equipment? Is there a size requirement to any of these rooms? Before designing any spaces, the interior designer must have conversations with the client, to answer these and other questions that will impact the overall configuration.

If it is a large organization with many people and subgroups, developing a list of spatial needs can be quite complex, requiring coordination and a thorough understanding of how the company functions to develop a program. Adjacencies, if collaborative effort between departments exists, and how best to support or even improve workflows can be discovered at this stage of the project.

Even with a residential client, understanding the ebb and flow of the individuals and the family has an impact on how, where, and what spaces need to be considered, as well as their sizes. This analytical, objective, data-gathering step enables the establishment of the goals of the client, which must be clearly stated, in order to set sights on a final project that will generate the desired results. Knowledge gaps that have been identified by the designers can be bridged at this point through research; at times, experts or consultants can be brought in. Initiating this groundwork sets expectations and a guide for the designer to follow so that the requirements of the client are met.

See also Process Part I, page 220

Design Student Yeri Caceres
Project Studio work

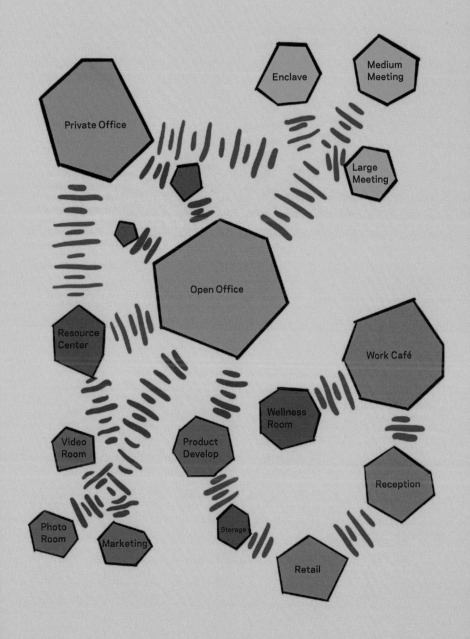

Placing spaces within the envelope of a building requires preparation and organization; there must be a general sense of their functions, how large the areas need to be, what the required or preferred adjacencies are, and a thorough understanding of building codes. People navigate from area to area through pathways, which act as connectors of spaces. This relationship between spaces and circulation has safety implications, as dead-end corridors, the distance to travel to an egress or safe exit staircase, or the number of doors needed for an assembly space must all adhere to the local jurisdiction's building codes.

    Interior designers are also responsible for arranging adjacencies to best accommodate workflows, as often described by the client. Commonly, because these areas have not been fully fleshed out and exact square footages have not been delineated, drawings such as bubble diagrams approximately show how the spaces relate to each other, circulation, and a loose configuration of the rooms. The designer must also keep in mind the constraints imposed not only by the building envelope but also by the client's budget, needs, and aspirational goals as established at the start of the process. Identifying rooms that are "front-of-house" or public-facing with visitors' access, which are "back-of-house" areas, and where all of them need to be placed requires study, as this pragmatic approach gives a broad outline of a plan that will be refined as the design progresses.

    Keeping this imprecise, to a degree, will help the client to recognize that this step is not actually the design but, rather, a broad picture of the zones' various functions. The one aspect of **space planning** that is critical is compliance with codes: for example, not creating dead-end corridors with lengths that exceed specified distances during this stage of the design process will ensure that considerable revisions are not required later.

See also Process Part I, page 220

The interior designer imposes a logic on the layout of the plan by arranging spaces and circulation in a very deliberate way. In fact, the artist Josef Albers noted, "To design is to plan and to organize, to order, to relate and to control. In short it embraces all means of opposing disorder and accident. Therefore, it signifies a human need and qualifies man's thinking and doing." For him, the absence of intention and rigor is the antithesis of design.

There are endless approaches to the **organization** of spaces. Some common ways include a grid with its many interactions or varieties, such as two intermeshed grids or a disrupted one; a centralized configuration exhibiting a dominant area surrounded by secondary spaces grouped around it; and a clustered organization containing spaces concentrated along a circulation route. An axial arrangement, which gathers rooms around a pathway or datum, creates a line. As with all things related to design, the selection of an overarching organization is never random; these strategies alone do not make a memorable space but, instead, it is the designer's underlying concept or intent made visible that provides an indelible experience of the interiors.

Organizing areas on multiple floors can be challenging, even for the seasoned designer; the client can be helped to appreciate these configurations with a series of color-coded diagrams that define elements such as location, size, adjacency, and shape of spaces for greater legibility.

Lastly, the organization of rooms may not be readily apparent upon the first visit. Only with a bird's-eye view of the floor plan is the entirety of the space visible—and this still does not provide the whole picture, as volume cannot be discerned in this way. The intended user cannot be expected to immediately comprehend the organization of spaces, but with repeat visits and curiosity one can begin to gather observations while inferring the logic and intent of the layout.

See also Process Part I, page 220

Design Student   Abbie McGrann
Project   Studio work

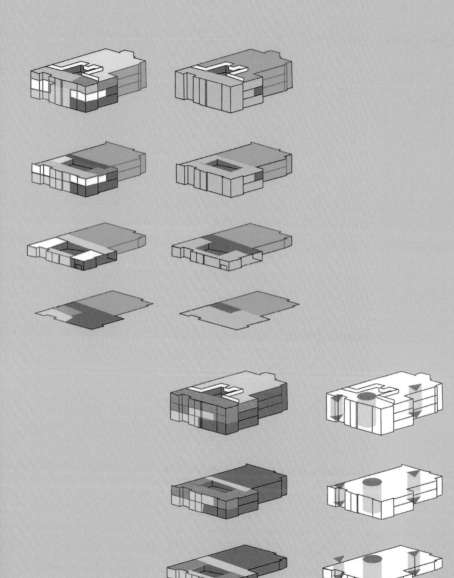

Circulation is the path or road used to get to one's destination; how to get there is wayfinding. Signage is one way to inform, if employed clearly and without ambiguity (think airports or train stations), but with some focused intention in the organization of spaces and paths—or circulation— the interior designer need not be reliant on signs alone. Clever design of circulation can tell users where they are and how to get to where they want to be.

The path does not need to be the Yellow Brick Road, but why not employ color to mark various zones or floors? Major intersections can be differentiated through the use of artwork or unique identifying design, such as landmarks, that provide recognition. A main artery path could be wider, more expansive, than secondary pathways, thus establishing a language and a hierarchy for the users to understand—similar to a main thoroughfare in a city, such as Pennsylvania Avenue in Washington, DC, or the Champs-Élysées in Paris. Where and how multiple corridors meet could be expressed as a node with radial paths branching outward. Lighting and different flooring materials can distinguish various zones to declare that a person is *here* and not *there*.

Most designs begin with the consideration of spaces or rooms, so wherever those are placed can determine the path or circulation to get there. Conversely, if one considers the layout of pathways, the spaces that are between them become the areas of activity. Circulation (negative space) and rooms (positive spaces) are different sides of the same coin. Showing this relationship as figure and ground can vividly represent spaces and circulation—and while plans are not depicted in this manner, interior designers contemplate this when considering the layout of a floor plan.

See also Accessibility, page 194

Design Student   Soorin Chung
Project   Studio work

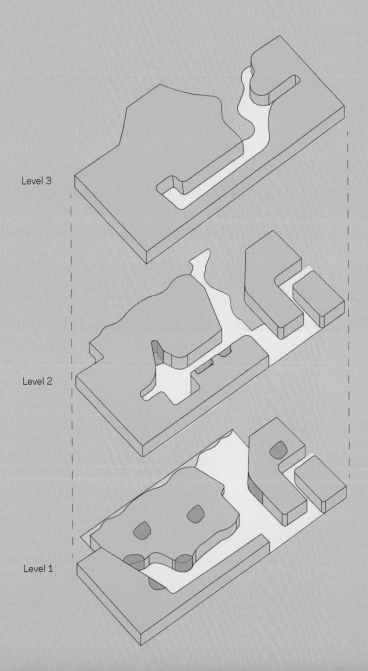

Level 3

Level 2

Level 1

Spaces can be shaped into any **geometry** imaginable, so why are straight walls and flat ceilings predominately used to configure rooms? Most materials, such as drywall (also known as Sheetrock or plasterboard) or glass, can be shaped to create arcs and curves, but it takes a great deal of effort and cost to bend materials that are rigid and fabricated as flat sheets. Square and rectangular spaces enable easy placement of furniture, which generally has straight edges (of course, there are exceptions, such as an oval coffee table) and can therefore be positioned directly alongside the walls.

Circular spaces can create a sense of harmony, with their gentle arcs and soft, organic lines. Depending on the circumference of the circle, materials that are rigid—such as baseboard along the bottom of the walls— need to be detailed carefully to ensure an accurate fit. This shape also demands the recognition of its center point as well as a design that highlights the perimeter. For example, the installation of a wood floor unavoidably establishes an orientation because of its grain and planks; if placed in a circular room, this would negate the non-directionality of the circle, unless wedge-shaped pieces radiated out from the center. Details such as this need to be executed carefully by both the designer and the builder of a circular space.

Despite the straight lines of a triangle, this shape promises to be the most problematic, with the vertices not being usable or easy to clean (especially if carpeted). With no right angles, the room can be quite challenging to furnish, and much of the equipment and furnishings would need to be away from the corners, wasting a lot of space. While not impossible, a triangular room defies most attempts at efficiency.

Interior designers need to understand how each geometry brings its own challenges, to effectively balance function and variety in a project

See also Form Making, page 66

Design Student   Becca Friedman
Project   Studio work

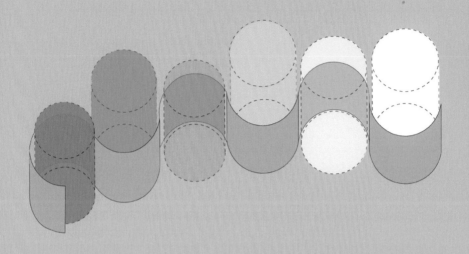

Light and dark, expansive and narrow, thin and wide, smooth and rough, small and large, ornate and plain, symmetrical and asymmetrical, old and new: these **contrasts** can be explored through the use of color, space, and materials, together or individually. Providing opposing experiences or elements that create tension can attract attention and "intensify each element's properties and produce a more dynamic expressiveness," as Francis D. K. Ching states in *Architecture: Form, Space, and Order*. Yet too much contrast can be jarring, and if there is an absence of unity it can create a dissonance threading through the entire experience.

In 1736, Italian architect and surveyor Giambattista Nolli was commissioned to construct a comprehensive plan of Rome: the result was a highly accurate and meticulously drawn map of the city. What Nolli delineated particularly clearly was the distinction between accessible civic spaces, shown as empty areas, and building mass, hatched in as solid, depicting zones that were not available to the public. These negative and positive spaces help the viewer to focus on this binary condition for a rapid understanding of the basic geography, even though it is magnificently complex and multilayered. Figure-ground representations showing public space inside and outside buildings in high contrast are still used today, and are known as Nolli maps.

The Museum of Cultures (MUDEC) in Milan by David Chipperfield exemplifies contrast through the design of a rigid, rectilinear architecture which contains within it a soft, curvilinear space. Visitors emerge from the ground level with its orthogonal walls into an organic, open area that forms a well-lit courtyard. This differentiation is heightened through the use of white vertical surfaces and ceiling, and a black floor. Because it is done with restraint, the contrast is not overwhelming but, rather, it all comes together to create a striking and memorable space.

See also Color Psychology, page 42

Design Student Soorin Chung
Project   Studio work

While the interior designer is constrained to create spaces within the envelope of a shell, or building, this should not result in simply dividing up areas with vertical walls from floor to ceiling, producing indiscriminate rooms and corridors. A popular alternative, the open floor plan, with its few walls and divisions, which facilitates the connectivity of spaces, certainly has merit—but the formation of distinguishable and discrete spaces (except for bathrooms and other areas where privacy is required) is not always evident. Composing experiences through the formation of **volumes** in various shapes or geometries that make memorable spaces is an appreciable facet of the discipline of interior design. Seeing this "architecture" or "building within building" is the reason why some refer to interior design as interior architecture.

Regardless of the name, designers are the "authors" of volumes, or spaces. The way in which they are imagined, collected, and organized to create a "society of rooms," as Estonian-born American architect Louis Kahn had it, is born from a concept. Articulating and defining volumes that have a distinct presence and promote a feeling of arrival can create a sense of hierarchy within a space, as well as significance or contrast.

Volume also relates to a sense of spaciousness, achieved through high ceilings, lighter-colored materials, and large openings that bring natural daylight into a space. It can also be interpreted as the negative space contained or carved out within a form, and possibly how sound travels through and around it, such as in a dome. The sizes of volumes are dependent on the architecture: an adaptive reuse warehouse with very high ceilings can easily accommodate two-story spaces, whereas this scenario would not be possible in most office buildings.

See also Form Making, page 66

Proportion and scale are often used interchangeably, but there are nuanced differences. Both pertain to the size of something, but the former is always concerned with the parts in relation to the entirety of an object. An example of this is the width of a person's face, which is approximately five times the width of their eye—anything much smaller or larger than this relationship or ratio (proportion) would look unusual, odd, or possibly unattractive, since the sense of harmony would be lost. The ancient Greeks were profoundly attentive to the pursuit of beauty through the rigid adherence to proportion, which is evidenced in the exquisite design of their temples.

Scale often involves proportion, though it can be a measurement that is not relative to anything. On a map, a graduated scale depicts a unit of measurement to represent a specific distance. The reduction of the map to a discernible scale is an invention that permits its very function; comprehension of one's neighborhood, city, or country—or even the world—would otherwise not be possible.

Similarly, in design scale refers to proportion between two sets of dimensions, such as between an original object and a drawing or model of it: interior designers implement scale to accurately represent reality through drawings in a reduced manner, as a way of conveying the sizes and dimensions of spaces to others for construction and comprehension.

Scale is also understood as a perception of the size of an object or space within its given context or in relation to human bodies. Very small light fixtures in an extremely large ballroom can appear "out of scale"; for the fixtures to be perceived as "correct," they must match the vastness of the space. French designer Philippe Starck often takes an ordinary object, such as a chair, and deliberately enlarges it so much that it creates a sense of drama and amusement. This playing with scale or oversizing elements gives an *Alice in Wonderland* feel to a space; adding whimsy never fails to delight the user.

See also Harmony, page 32

Drawings are one of the most fundamental ways in which design intentions are communicated to others, while simultaneously allowing the interior designer to comprehend any complex construct. Depending on the audience and purpose, the word can refer to many different types of documentation.

At the start of the design process, the drawings produced may not resemble anything that is recognizable, but this very act of depiction becomes part of ideas unfolding, which generates a vision. Engaging in this manner allows for a connection between the eye, hand, and brain, thus forming a feedback loop; ideas are "pulled" from the mind—another definition of the verb "to draw." The tangible documentation generated allows the designer to assess and critically review the images while retaining a kind of testimony of the process. At times, working through a problem—be it a detail or organizing complex relationships between parts through illustrations—can be effectively accomplished by taking pencil to paper.

To assist the client in realizing the spaces that the interior designer has envisioned, rendered perspective drawings are often produced to give life to the floor plans, which alone cannot communicate the entire design. The specification of materials on walls and floors, the heights of spaces, the lighting, furniture, and so on are difficult for many people to envisage without a visual, such as the perspective drawing. It also depicts how one experiences space, hence its capacity to help the viewer imagine how it would feel to inhabit that area.

Plans, sections, elevations, and details used to communicate to the contractor are found in a set of construction drawings. While they may be viewed as dry and technical, without these "instructions" or, to use an old phrase, blueprints, the contractor would not be able to build the space according to the vision of the interior designer and the consultants who contributed to the project.

See also Ideating: Sketching, page 64

Attempting to visualize a design from a two-dimensional perspective or floor plan is vastly different from viewing a three-dimensional representation of space to scale. While most interior design firms do not generate them for clients, as a beginner design student, assembling spaces with one's hands enables the understanding of how volumes and forms are literally created. **Three-dimensional models** are an effective tool to communicate design ideas, and while sketching is also another vehicle with which to do this, for many, transforming ideas in the mind into illustrations can be extremely difficult and unsatisfying, especially if one lacks the ability to draw. Many are eager to rush to a computer for this task, but while software can execute some functions it severely limits one's ability to be creative. Tools do not promote innovative thinking; they are a means to document or produce an interior designer's vision.

Computer-generated images are two-dimensional—no matter how sophisticated they appear, the views are static; "exploring" them isn't possible in the same way that a physical model can be picked up and rotated. Finnish architect and educator Juhani Pallasmaa noted, "Even in the age of computer-aided design and virtual modeling, physical models are incomparable aids in the design process…[t]he three-dimensional material model speaks to the hand and the body as powerfully as to the eye."

People continually inhabit space, but most are rarely in a position to create or understand it in a way that is internalized and ingrained in their ways of thinking, like an interior designer can. Constructing a model requires a person to address and understand the three-dimensional spatial arrangements; all planes, surfaces, and so on can be explored in a way that drawings cannot express or wholly explain. They can also facilitate the design process to an end; typically, these study models, made with chipboard or cardboard, are extremely useful to work through ideas or even discover solutions that were not attainable through sketching or thinking alone.

See also Form Making, page 66

5.0 —— Project Types

Home is where the heart is, as the old saying goes. And it couldn't be truer, as no project type is more personal than **residential**. This includes detached, attached, stacked, single-family or multi-family housing, wherever a person or family (however one defines it) *lives*.

    While designers can be hired directly by a client, in larger-scale residential projects, such as new buildings, interior designers will collaborate with architects from the start. Throughout the process, designers are involved in every aspect, such as organizing the floor plan(s) of required spaces; specifying wall and door types, including hardware; selecting kitchen appliances, bathroom fixtures, and plumbing fittings; choosing the finishes for floors, walls, and ceilings, as well as cabinetry built-ins and countertop materials; and picking furniture, accessories, and even art to create a fully cohesive project. It's a myth that only the very wealthy can afford this service, as clients of many income levels seek out designers just as they would any other professional. There are even designers that focus on small apartments and tiny homes, as well as others that offer virtual consulting by the hour.

    For clients who work with designers, the selection of one can almost be akin to dating, as several may need to be interviewed to find the best connection. For the designer, the first step in the collaborative relationship is to understand the user. The more information shared, the closer the interior design can mold the interior toward the client. Designers modify the floor plan by removing and adding non-load-bearing walls (note that the removal of load-bearing, or structural, walls must be approved by a registered architect or structural engineer) and lead all the decisions including follow-through, which includes generating purchase orders and construction administration.

    Furthermore, interior designers coordinate with architects, engineers, and construction trades (as the project warrants), and facilitate the final installation. Clients can be hands-off until the moment they walk into their finished dream home.

See also Artwork, page 150

Designer   Bestor Architecture
Project   Private residence
Location   Bend, OR, US

There are reasons why people want their bedrooms and baths to look and feel like a hotel—think white fluffy towels and thick down comforters. **Hotels** embody the feeling of being away from the stresses of daily life; who wouldn't want to feel as if they are on a permanent vacation? Even the hotel lobby has evolved into a public "living room" and become a popular gathering spot for both guests and non-guests. It is a "third place," which is defined as somewhere outside of the home or office in which people gather to work or socialize.

Hotel design, coming under the hospitality umbrella, is about creating a specific environment for the user, mainly on a temporary basis (although who wouldn't want to live at the Plaza Hotel in New York like the eponymous Eloise in Kay Thompson's classic children's books?). Interior designers work with hotel owners and management to create a unique experience based on many factors including programmatic requirements, square footage, context, budget, and hotel branding/philosophy—whether a hotel, motel, boutique, or chain. The above factors must be researched to create a strong design concept that will carry throughout the hotel, from the lobby through the corridors and into the rooms.

Incorporating the greatest number of rooms within a tight footprint while maintaining the idea of an oasis can be challenging— doubly challenging once you add to that functional, technical, and code requirements. And as travel trends evolve, designs must evolve, too. The Cornell Center for Hospitality Research states that millennials will soon represent 50 percent of all travelers in the United States: this means designers need to consider how to keep the attention of a generation of tech-savvy adventurers who hold experiences in high regard, and who are not afraid to share their negative as well as their positive impressions on various forms of social media.

See also Programming, page 76

Designer   Space Copenhagen
Project   11 Howard
Location   New York, NY, US

As celebrity chefs and self-described "foodies" show no signs of fading away, **restaurants** continue to be a wonderful place to break bread with friends and family. Add to the experience of delicious food an interior to match, and a successful restaurant is made. When designing spaces for eating, the type of cuisine is often the impetus for the concept; however, it is important to note that while the food can be the point of inspiration, it is not a theme. Designers do not have to create a miniature Rome to serve Italian food.

Once a space is selected, the interior designer interviews the client to begin the programming phase, which is based on the needs of all the users—diners, management, and staff. Adjacency diagrams are a tool that is used to indicate what spaces need to be next to, near, or far from one other. Then the floor plan evolves by balancing the needs of the restaurateur, such as table types and sizes, bar and bar seating, hostess and service areas, private dining rooms, commercial kitchen access and needs, and number and type of restrooms. Designers also think about details such as how to create a lighting experience that makes diners look good (hint: this is often achieved by a strong dimming system).

Since diners are generally there to talk as well as eat, designers must pay specific attention to acoustics. Too many hard surfaces will cause sound to bounce, creating a frustrating experience for any conversationalist. Other critical factors, such as durability of finishes and ease of maintenance, must be factored in when designing, since many restaurants have a quick turnover rate with constant use. It's a lengthy design process, even for the simplest eating establishment. Coffee shops have also become "third places," where people come to drink coffee, meet friends, and do work. When food and interiors connect, it's magic. Bon Appetit!

See also Comfort, page 180

Designer   Space Copenhagen
Project   108
Location   Copenhagen, Denmark

American artist Barbara Kruger's bold 1987 artwork Untitled (*I shop therefore I am*) displays these words as a strong graphic statement about consumerism. This thought-provoking piece about material goods in society hasn't slowed down the rate of public consumption. With the advent of online shopping, one could say it's only sped up.

Remote **retail** has many advantages, such as shopper convenience, potentially global visibility for the brand, and no brick-and-mortar costs for the retailer. Yet there are still shoppers who value the in-store experience and the process of directly engaging with a product. That's where the interior designer comes in. They work with retailers and visual merchandisers to create spaces that define the brand philosophy and successfully display the product, with the goal of making sales and increasing profit.

Interior designers must understand the psychology of customer behavior, starting at the store's entry—also known as the decompression zone—so that the space sets the tone without overwhelming the shopper. They consider how shoppers move through the space (grid or loop layout; free-flow or forced path); how products will be displayed or viewed using sight lines and focal points; how the items will be lit, whether general or accent lighting; how users will engage with the products using displays, mirrors,
and dressing rooms; how to incorporate a visible and accessible POS (point of sale); and where to locate back-of-house requirements such as storage.

It's a lot to consider...but if it brings sales for the client and happiness to the shopper, then designers are doing something right. Here's to a little retail therapy.

See also Lighting, page 146

Designer   Neri&Hu
Project   Lab by Lane Crawford
Location   Hong Kong, China

Once upon a time many years ago, the most visited museum in the world was overcrowded and in disrepair. In 1988, a Chinese-American architect named I. M. Pei designed a pyramid of glass to house a new entry, which became an icon of France and of contemporary architecture. Less discussed, however, was the renovation of the submerged entrance below the pyramid, which delineated three access points with clear circulation paths that led to the galleries, restrooms, and service spaces, which were previously lacking. And while the exterior remains iconic visually, it is the interior that functions for nine million users annually—as well as curatorial, exhibit, operations, and maintenance staff. And so, the story of the Louvre in Paris has a happy ending.

Cultural spaces include all types of interiors that engage the public in the arts, which broadly encompasses art, design, theater, film, dance, and music. A key element for any of these spaces, especially those of larger scale—as seen in the example of the Louvre—is wayfinding, or the systems used for the visitor to navigate successfully through a space. Visitors engage in cultural spaces to be educated, inspired, and entertained, and the interior design has a strong impact on the experience.

San Francisco-based architect Art Gensler founded his namesake firm in 1965, and it has remained a design powerhouse for decades. Gensler was forward-thinking in approaching architecture with an "inside-out" approach, which emphasized the user experience within the building. The importance of the interior was communicated to his clients and helped to legitimize the interior design profession. Even today, the Gensler firm approaches all its cultural projects with these ideas as well as with the goals of equity and inclusivity—and the notion that public spaces should be for everyone, no matter the demographic, income, age, or ability. These cultural spaces make all users feel welcome. Thank you, Art Gensler.

See also Circulation, page 82

Designer   Gensler
Project   International Center of Photography
Location   New York, NY, US

By far the most famous educator was the Chinese philosopher Confucius, whose teachings from around 500 BCE about kindness still resonate today. Ideally, young schoolchildren will learn about honesty and integrity in a physical environment that supports these views. And while there are, sadly, wide discrepancies in educational opportunity among populations, when given the chance interior designers can create dynamic, innovative spaces that support, encourage, and motivate learning—and make a real impact on the **learning** process.

With the advent of digital technology and the ubiquity of the Internet, students have shorter attention spans than before; therefore, interior designers seek to create dynamic spaces that utilize active, hands-on learning. This includes a variety of breakout areas within larger spaces and the selection of well-designed, ergonomic furniture to encourage both movement and interaction with other students. Studies show that natural light and natural elements drawing on biophilia also have a positive effect within the academic environment, while acoustics, air quality, and ventilation control are important for spaces intended for close conversation, discussion, and collaboration. School is a place to feel safe, and shared spaces encourage students to study and socialize.

The Bauhaus, a modernist arts and design school in Germany founded by Walter Gropius in 1919, encouraged a sense of community with oversize stairways and landings, so that students and faculty could connect between classes. With such connections in mind, interior designers look to provide inclusive, flexible, and healthy spaces where every student wants to be, from kindergarten through graduate school.

See also Sensory Balance, page 50, and Heating, Ventilation + Air Conditioning, page 188

Designer   Design, Bitches
Project   9 Dots
Location   Los Angeles, CA, US

The once standard nine-to-five office job is becoming a rare beast. As employees seek flexibility in their work schedule and technology allows people to work from anywhere, the design of office space has been forced to adapt, especially since companies looking to attract talent have no choice but to move away from traditional, hierarchical offices and endless cubicles. This doesn't mean the office is dead: on the contrary, interior designers are creating new and exciting **workplaces** that encourage in-person utilization and increase equity. One thing is clear: employees want to work in a space that both looks and feels good. Both can be achieved by balancing a strong visual concept with a variety of environments, so that employees have physical spaces to fit their needs at any given time.

Employees no longer need to sit at one desk all day, and offices are designed to encourage and facilitate movement, providing areas that are dependent on the task (this is also referred to as activity-based work). To create innovative and ergonomic workstations, smaller meeting spaces, and larger conference rooms, designers may collaborate with furniture dealers —for example, MillerKnoll and Steelcase—to customize individual workstations as well as furniture for collaborative settings. Rather than having an assigned space, employees are often a part of a desk-sharing system, which eliminates empty spaces and maximizes usage. Designers also create varying-sized breakout rooms, social spaces, and amenities such as a community kitchen (also called a pantry).

Many of the same elements discussed in other project types— proxemics, natural daylight, biophilia, circulation, air quality, and thermal comfort—are all considered when designing for the office. And, as in other public spaces, textiles, furniture, and finishes are required to be of commercial grade to account for heavier usage. There may be an option to work from home a few days a week, but with a visually stunning office space that enhances collaboration and productivity, who would want to?

See also Ergonomics, page 36, and FF+E, page 142

Designer   Shepley Bulfinch
Project   Shepley Bulfinch Office
Location   Boston, MA, US

Healthcare is a broad term that includes hospitals, clinics, doctor and dentist surgeries, mental institutions, hospices, and nursing homes. Unlike a spa, many users are in these kinds of spaces not by choice but by necessity. Along with patients, doctors, nurses, and other operational staff and visitors such as family and friends create a type of village. **Healthcare**, a large and growing field of design, is a project type that provides meaningful work to interior designers who want to make a difference in the world of healing others.

The California-based Center for Health Design defines evidence-based design as "the process of basing decisions about the built environment on credible research to achieve the best possible outcomes." Using research to create spaces that are proven to work for the users is a demonstrated way for design to play a role in the treatment and recovery of patients. This includes the consideration of space planning, noise, privacy, and cleanliness. Wayfinding is crucial for patients who are visually impaired or who suffer from dementia. Materials used for components such as flooring, walls, furniture, and textiles must meet various standards to not be slippery or spread germs. All elements within healthcare must be hygienic and easy to maintain. And acoustics plays a large role in spaces with machinery, which can be noisy and stressful. Incorporating art and the concept of biophilia has also been proven to lift spirits and help people heal faster.

Community-centered design focuses on the connection of people within their communities with the resources to live healthy, happy lives. Within some healthcare facilities, anxiety and long wait times for appointments can intimidate those who need care most. Interior designers are challenged to design interiors with a level of sensitivity that result in spaces that feel welcoming, safe, and calm. Through interviews and programming, as well as researching the health specialty one is designing for, designers understand the type of care and the needs of those who use it.

See also Space Planning, page 78, and Codes, page 186

Designer   Brandon Haw Architecture
Project   New York Dermatology Group
Location   New York, NY, US

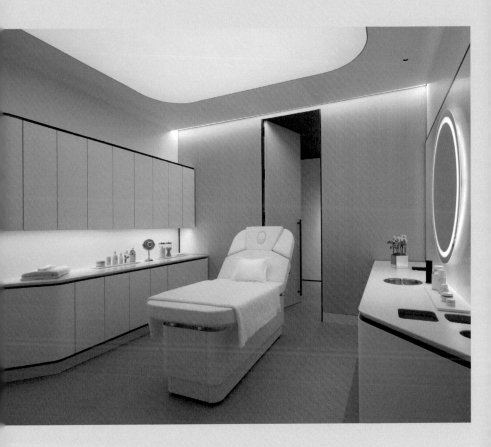

The word "goop" used to mean a sticky glob of gooey paste; now, it's an award-winning **wellness** platform that offers a wide array of information and an online store selling vitamins, non-toxic makeup, and organic clothing. An offshoot of healthcare, wellness is about maintaining mental and physical health through practices such as meditation, yoga, Pilates, fitness, and healthy eating.

Interior designers create spaces for wellness to encourage the user's success in the space (energetic gyms, blissful spas). Understanding the psychology of exercise and how the environment can encourage movement is essential. Using this knowledge, designers focus on the feel of space through the design concept, materiality, and color theory, while considering proxemics, anthropometrics, and ergonomics so that the interiors are inclusive and comfortable for everyone.

For a yoga studio, a designer may start with the size of a mat, and use it to determine the size of the room, but the spatial needs are much more complex since these areas need to encourage both movement and relaxation. Functional requirements such as circulation, thermal comfort, air quality, acoustics, and lighting are balanced with user behavior and, often, a minimalist aesthetic. Biophilia is prevalent in the wellness sphere; many spas incorporate water features and natural materials to connect with nature—even in urban areas. Treatment rooms need ample space for activities such as massage, acupuncture, facials, and therapy. Gyms focus on the layout and safety of fitness equipment, as well as the functional aspects of locker and shower rooms.

Every subset of wellness has its own checklist of necessities as each space creates a sense of mindfulness while still stimulating the user. The goal is to tap into the spiritual, emotional, and physical through the senses. Time to light that organic candle.

See also Biophilia, page 48 and Wood, page 120

Designer   BKSK Architects
Project   1 Great Jones Alley, Movement Studio
Location   New York, NY, US

While a destination may be exotic, there is always a journey to get there —which could include a highway rest stop, a bus or train station, a boat terminal, or an airport. The people who use these interiors are transient, as users aim to move through these spaces rapidly to get to their final destination. Hungry, tired travelers want their needs met quickly, and they want to be in control of the process. A well-designed space can enhance the experience and provide a sense of relaxation, as many people **travel** for pleasure; and even those on the move for business crave a low-stress experience.

The challenge is to create clear, functional spaces with efficient wayfinding for a large demographic of users who range in age, ability, and background. Specifically, signage needs to be large and graphic to span languages and age groups. Movement throughout transit areas needs to be intuitive and uncomplicated since users are on specific schedules to meet departure times. Most of the public spaces in these project types incorporate food, retail, restrooms, ticketing, security, waiting areas, and departure and arrival gates.

Wayfinding, comfort, durability, maintenance, and budget are all important factors, but how the spaces feel can change the experience for a traveler. Designers are challenged to meet all of these requirements including flexibility, since at certain times of the day there may be smaller or larger numbers of travelers. And many people travel alone, so safety is a considerable factor which needs to be integrated into the design so as not to alarm travelers…Who wants giant security cameras to intrude on their journey?

A strong design concept, incorporating natural light, color, pattern, and texture in a skillful way to create comfortable interiors, plays a large part in reducing travel anxiety. The 1960s jet-set era of dressing up for air travel is long gone, but the interiors can still be inviting.

See also Circulation, page 82, and Accessibility, page 194

Designer   SOM
Project   Washington Dulles International Airport
Location   Dulles, VA, US

6.0 ⎯⎯ Materiality

Whether it's a veneer or solid piece, **wood** has a natural warmth that attracts interior designers to its use. Because they are taken from a living, growing organism, the color, grain pattern, and durability of two pieces of wood from separate trees of the same species, or even from different parts of the same log, will never match exactly. With so many stains or finishes that can be applied, the results are nearly limitless.

Architect Louis Kahn was fond of employing wood with concrete, sensitively recognizing that a maple handrail on which to rest one's hand is much more hospitable than cold concrete. Thanks to its relative softness, wood eventually shows the effects of time and use, making it feel welcoming and worn in, like a favorite leather jacket. The art of matching flitches (lengthwise slices of log) or veneers can be executed with incredible richness: the ways in which they can be arranged is quite varied, since the cutting process determines the appearance of the grain, as does the species. Wood's versatility—panels may be used for walls, cabinetry, doors, furniture, floors, or ceilings—can equally create an upscale or a modest appearance. Glued together to fabricate laminated trusses, wood is strong enough to mean that it is often exploited for structural uses as well.

Some species of wood, because of their natural beauty, fall victim to their own popularity. Because of heightened demand, they can be difficult to obtain and, in a vicious circle, this rarity drives further exploitation. Wood, as a natural material, takes years to grow and mature; high demand can quickly lead to depletion of forests and unsustainable harvesting of such resources. Deforestation, damage to the lands of Indigenous peoples, and illegal logging are examples of the destructive impact a sought-after material can have on the environment. When specifying for a project, designers have a responsibility for the ethical acquisition of wood as a material for interior spaces.

See also Biophilia, page 48

6.1 —— Materiality

Designer	Clive Wilkinson Architects
Project	Private residence
Location	Los Angeles, CA, US

Bricks have been in continuous use for the construction of buildings since approximately 7000 BCE. Evidence of the modular material can be traced to present-day Syria and Turkey, where mud blocks were dried in the sun and hardened prior to use. With the adoption of the kiln to fire bricks, cooler climate regions were able to manufacture them without relying on the sun's heat. Bricks are typically found on the exterior of buildings, and are not frequently specified as an interior material. However, the decision to expose an existing structure of brick construction in a room can appear to peel back layers of the past while blurring the distinction between inside and outside.

 With its uniformity, modularity, and spacing dictated by the thickness of the mortar, brick has a distinctive texture, which can show the age of the construction beautifully. Even old or slightly damaged brick, with its roughness and tactility, contrasts wonderfully with smooth drywall (plasterboard) or any new insertion. Old brick exudes a sense of history, and the color, typically a rusty red (although there are many varieties, from gray to tan to orange hues), brings a sense of warmth to a room. While a single, universal standard dimension does not exist—sizes vary from country to country—the common feature is the ability of a brick to fit into a single hand. The way bricks are laid—known as their bond, or pattern—is as important as the way they are oriented. Bricks in a vertical position are soldiers; stretchers are placed horizontally; a stretcher rotated 90 degrees is a header. These three orientations are used to produce many variations and subtle patterns that are revealed to a discerning eye.

 For many of the houses that the American architect Frank Lloyd Wright designed, his material of choice was brick. In particular, the long, horizontal lines of brick emphasized his concept of where sky meets ground as "the true earth line of human life," or the American prairie. Few recent designers have been able to employ this material as beautifully as Wright.

See also Sensory Pattern, page 44

Designer   Neri&Hu
Project   Design Republic Home
Location   Shanghai, China

Stone bestows a sense of monumentality on any setting—after all, there is an understanding that something is permanent when it is "set in stone." The ancient Egyptians were acutely conscious of this when they created monuments that pushed the boundaries of what people could construct. The great pyramids of Giza, standing strong through more than 4,500 years of human history, were constructed using millions of tons of stone, which even time has not been able to erode into oblivion.

While specifying stone for interiors is a more modest undertaking, it always elevates the appearance of a space. Veins, or lines of crystalized minerals, may course through it like rivers, emphasizing the substance's organic quality and uniqueness. There are no repeat patterns: this is the calling card of real stone that hasn't been manufactured and stamped with a veining pattern in an attempt to mimic the timeless character of the material. Cutting stone to highlight any veining and matching the lines to create an organic pattern is similar to the way wood veneers are matched up and placed on vertical panels. Stone can be used for flooring, although designers must be mindful of the coefficient of friction, or the rating that measures the slipperiness of a material's surface. The lower the number, the more perilous it is to walk on it; a higher number denotes a greater slip resistance or friction.

Countertops for kitchens and bathrooms, as well as sinks and basins, are common ways for interior designers to use stone. It can be finished in various ways, including polishing, honing, and planing; depending on the application and the desired appearance, the treatments create very different effects. Permanence, solidity, and a sense of monumentality— stone continues to evoke these timeless qualities.

See also Kitchen + Bathroom, page 154

Designer   Space Copenhagen
Project   Private residence
Location   Skodsborg, Denmark

Light fixtures, door hardware, guardrails, handrails, stairs, woven mesh in elevator cabs, screens, dividers, ceiling panels, furniture, door frames—these are just some of the ways in which **metal** is used in the design of everyday objects and spaces. Because of its ubiquity, one hardly notices many of these applications. Recall the last time you touched a door handle, and chances are it was metal. Its strength lies in its durability. In high-traffic areas, such as a public restroom, a metal kickplate at the door's lower portion ensures that it does not appear shabby over time through the constant contact of people's shoes.

Conversely, metal can bring a glint and a touch of glamor to an otherwise sober space. Perforated panels and screens cut with laser accuracy can divide spaces, enabling light and views through. This, however, also allows the transmission of sound; in a space where multiple hard surfaces are adjacent, metal panels need to be considered carefully to avoid negatively impacting the acoustical quality. A decorative, woven wire mesh using various thicknesses and types of metal can yield immense variations and options, acting as a curtain or barrier but with a toughness that fabric does not offer. In the photograph shown, thin brass bars are welded to create three-dimensional structures—an ethereal frame that simultaneously separates and connects spaces visually and acoustically.

Different finishes produce myriad results: a high polish can provide a mirror-like reflection while a brushed or satin finish is more forgiving, masking fingerprints and smudges. Stainless steel, chrome, nickel, and aluminum are "white" or cool metals; warmer or yellow metals are brass and bronze. Copper, with its orange tones, stands on its own and, as it ages, develops a blue-green patina. Whichever metals are selected, they always give a refined and elegant appearance to an interior environment.

See also Hardware, page 152

6.4 ——— Materiality

Designer	Neri&Hu
Project	Sulwhasoo Flagship Store
Location	Seoul, South Korea

Precast or poured **concrete**, also known as in situ or cast in place, is certainly one of the most ubiquitous building materials. It was used extensively by the Romans, who built aqueducts and the sublime dome of the Pantheon—at 142 feet (43 meters) across, still the world's largest unsupported unreinforced-concrete dome. In the modern world, the humble material creates an immense variety of structures in the built environment, from parking garages to museums (see the British architect David Chipperfield's elegant reconstruction of Berlin's Neues Museum).

Concrete has a spartan, sober appearance, with its light gray color and heavy presence, but depending on its use, it can also lend a refined and serene effect. Perhaps some of the best examples of the material employed in this manner are by Japanese architect Tadao Ando, whose works have the presence of introspective and meditative spaces. A softness is expressed and because it is so finely cast, one almost forgets that what is seen is concrete. As it molds into whatever form it is poured, concrete has a versatile plasticity that can create a unique, sinuous shape or banal, modular slabs or walls for rapid, tilt-up construction. While its great advantage is its ability to withstand compression, it works best in harmony with steel, which provides tensile strength. Used together, they constitute reinforced concrete.

A coarseness can be created, made by the concrete seeping between the planks or boards, exposing separations. In other cases, the grain from the plywood form leaves behind a mark or imprint, generating a texture. A completely different approach is to fabricate a seamless appearance, making the surface smooth and giving a monolithic feel, characterizing concrete as a mass with a sculptural quality. With care and planning, concrete as an element in the design of an interior can be used to express richness or starkness, depending on the designer's intent.

See also Form Making, page 66

By covering surfaces in a variety of colors, materials, and textures, **tiles** have the ability to animate a space. Tiles can be made out of various materials according to function, including ceiling tiles, which are typically 2 x 2 foot (60 x 60 cm) acoustic squares set inside a suspended metal grid; carpet tiles, which are modular pieces of carpet rather than a single continuous roll; and roof tiles made of asphalt or clay. Tiles are also made of glass, stone, metal, and, perhaps the most common, ceramic and porcelain.

While not always discernible, there are differences between porcelain and ceramic tiles. Think of porcelain like a carrot—its color is not only on the surface but throughout the entire section of the vegetable. Ceramic is more like a radish—the red is only on the outer portion and, once you cut through it, the interior is seen to be white. The glaze of a ceramic tile can be chipped away to reveal a different color, just below the surface.

In terms of durability, porcelain is better: being fired at a higher temperature for a longer time than ceramic tile makes it less fragile and less water absorbent than ceramic. Because of porcelain's ability to withstand more wear and tear, it's commonly found on floors or any high-use surfaces and can also be specified for outdoor use. For bathroom walls, kitchen backsplashes, or other locations that aren't subjected to excessive use, ceramic tiles are a good fit. Tiles protect the walls from excessive moisture, are fire resistant, and can be kept very clean.

The beauty of both materials is that there is an infinite number of ways to create patterns, textures, and designs, thanks to the myriad shapes and colors that are available. Grout colors, while not as varied as tile, can also influence the look by matching or contrasting with the colors of the tiles. A contrast-color grout will accentuate the shape or configuration of the tiles, while a lighter color will blend in for a monochromatic look.

See also Pattern, page 44

Glass is seemingly everywhere in the built environment. Modern skyscrapers are literally sheathed or draped with it—the term "curtain wall" refers to the way that glass (or some other nonstructural cladding) hangs from the frame of a building. The transparency of glass, its defining attribute, provides visual connection between the inside and the outside of a structure, while providing protection from the elements to those on the inside. Glassmaking was known to many ancient cultures but the use of glass in windows took off only after around 100 CE, when the Romans discovered how to make clear glass. A millennium later, stained glass was widely employed in Gothic cathedrals across Northern Europe, these jewel-toned windows creating sublime spaces brought to life with multicolored light.

Interior applications today include areas where varying degrees of visual access and daylight is desired, such as conference rooms and private offices, where options to use glass include doors, sidelights, and clerestory windows. Internal rooms created with glass walls can make occupants feel as though they are in a fishbowl (not to mention, there's no place to hide a mess), although sandblasting or acid-etching glass can create differing degrees of opacity. Alternatively, interior designers can specify Mylar film (a thin polyester film) to cover the glass; this can easily be laser-cut with any design imaginable, and once it is adhered to the surface some privacy from passing stares is restored. Disadvantages of glass include its limited function as an acoustic buffer, and the fact that it easily gets marked with oil from hands.

Glass with a pattern imprinted on the surface is called figured glass. Wired glass, also called safety glass, has a wire net embedded in it to hold it together in the event of breakage. Glass blocks are molded in half-sections with the two pieces heat-sealed together; they are installed like bricks with joints reinforced every two or three courses. The use of glass blocks peaked in the 1980s; however, they are still specified occasionally for a very distinct, retro look.

See also Connection to Nature, page 176

Designer   Neri&Hu
Project   HKU Shanghai Center
Location   Shanghai, China

Mirrors have a much-needed and practical application (consider getting ready in the morning without using one), but they also provide a bit of sparkle in a room with their "shiny object" allure. A simple way to lend the appearance of a more spacious and light-filled space, they additionally create points of interest. They seem to expand the proportions of any enclosure and generate the impression of a grand room. Mirrors' shapes are limited only by the imagination and they can be framed in endless ways.

Before they were made with glass, mirrors were small, polished disks of metal that were rare acquisitions. Venetian craftsmen in the 16th century mastered the art of applying reflective materials such as tin and mercury onto glass. So valued were their techniques that they were concealed by the craftsmen, who were sworn to secrecy, with the threat of death preventing them from disclosing the process to anyone. This effective monopoly forced France to develop its own glassmaking capacities, rather than propping up Venice's economy through the purchase of luxury items in massive quantities.

Louis XIV established the Royal Mirror Glass Factory in 1665, which became Saint-Gobain; it is still manufacturing glass today, in addition to other construction materials. In 1678, the factory produced the glass mirror surfaces for the Hall of Mirrors in the Palace of Versailles, intended to rival what the Venetians were fabricating. The sheer number (357) and size of the mirrors put on such ostentatious display was proof of the Sun King's wealth and of France's ability to do what the Venetians could do—but even better. By modern standards, the Hall of Mirrors is impressive; imagine what a breathtaking and ethereal experience it would have been, viewing the reflections of the gardens and the gilded interiors, illuminated by candles.

See also Accessories, page 148

Designer   Bates Masi + Architects
Project   Private residence
Location   Water Mill, NY, US

A **textile**'s ability to hold up through constant use is measured after applying deliberate abrasions (sometimes called "double rubs") through one of two abrasion test methods: Wyzenbeek or Martindale. While they are not exactly comparable, each tells an interior designer how a particular textile will wear in various settings as well as how it can be cleaned or maintained. Other factors to consider include its construction and composition, whether it uses man-made strands (such as polypropylene or rayon), natural fibers (such as cotton, silk, or wool), or both. In a healthcare setting, textiles that can endure repeated cleanings and have high stain resistance need to be specified, to resist bacteria growth while withstanding constant use. Some textiles attain a third-party certification, substantiating the manufacturer's claim of sustainability.

In addition to aesthetics, multiple factors are weighed by the interior designer prior to the final selection of a textile. Its appropriateness for the task in mind, such as upholstering furniture or banquette seating, and its durability are criteria that must first be resolved. If the fabric is patterned, the interior designer must be aware of where and how the pattern will be oriented and repeated (on the back of a sofa, for example), in addition to identifying the location and alignment of seams. Designers also consider the use of textiles for acoustic comfort: fabric-wrapped panels on walls can mitigate noise and at the same time add color to a space.

After sitting on a plastic or wood surface for a few hours, one will most certainly appreciate the tactile benefits of an upholstered seat. The impact of textiles cannot be overstated, especially since the user's experience of them is generally mediated through the sense of touch.

See also Comfort, page 180

Many interior partitions, or walls, are composed of drywall (Sheetrock, plasterboard) that form rooms with straight, perpendicular walls, or hallways. But what if the design aesthetic leans away from the norm? Molding and shaping a supporting structure or formwork with materials such as fiberglass creates a frame that can be clad with a **nontraditional** element to create radical spaces. The use of technology, such as 3D printers and digital fabrication, allows interior designers more freedom to explore dynamic forms and to bring to life a vision of fluid shapes that goes beyond the application of curved and sweeping lines. This would have impressed even the artists and designers of the Art Nouveau style of the late 19th century.

The push for more eco-conscious materials has seen the rise of inventions and explorations that pursue a smaller carbon footprint from the construction and design industry. Reusing waste or byproduct, such as sawdust or fly ash (from coal combustion), while not common, is slowly gaining traction. Even crop waste, such as seed husks or plant stalks, can be incorporated into substrates, replacing medium-density fiberboard (MDF) for the fabrication of cabinets. Rather than discarding the broken bits of bran and straw that are generated during the process of gathering and processing rice, these can be captured and used to create flooring that substitutes for plastic. Mycelium, the portion of a fungus composed of a diaphanous network of branching rootlike structures, is 100 percent renewable and biodegradable—and is surprisingly durable, allowing it to be used for flooring and insulated wall panels. Plant-based textiles and "pleathers" that mimic animal hides also contribute to this wonderful plethora of innovative substances. With each discovery, designers move the field forward, altering perceptions by rethinking old methods and inventing new ones, exploring raw materials that have never been examined or regarded as usable before.

See also Materials, page 166

Designer   Karim Rashid
Project   Fun Factory
Location   Munich, Germany

7.0 —— Products

A common term used in commercial interior design is FF+E, which stands for furniture, fixtures, and equipment. This includes all the items that are outside of the architectural scope, and which the interior designer specifies, orders, and coordinates for installation. Think of these as things that are not part of the architectural shell or connected to the structural, mechanical, electrical, or plumbing components of a building. So anything that "moves" is considered part of the FF+E package, as well as items that are installed but not permanent (such as floating shelving or a chandelier).

Interior designers can also specify appliances, plumbing fixtures and fittings, and hardware—more on these later—but the contractor and subcontractors typically order and install them. **Furniture** is movable, and includes the obvious such as chairs, tables, and upholstered items, as well as rugs, table and floor lamps, accessories, and even art. **Fixtures** are items that are attached to the building, but on which the building is not reliant, such as built-in banquettes, ceiling-mounted or pendant lighting, and window treatments: such items are connected to a floor, wall, or ceiling, but they are cosmetically attached and can be removed easily. **Equipment** is plugged in, but also movable, and consists of items such as computers, copiers, and other electronics.

For commercial projects, such as workplaces, the FF+E costs are significant when assessing the value of a company. Designers select and specify products with the design concept in mind, as well as considering codes and industry standards. In spaces such as healthcare, additional factors such as flammability, durability, sustainability, and maintenance will affect FF+E specifications. Either way, the inclusion of these elements is a big part of interior design, and there are even positions in firms that focus solely on this part of the project.

See also Retail, page 104

Designer   Studio Sofield
Project   Tom Ford
Location   Beverly Hills, CA, US

The Swiss furniture company Vitra sells iconic chairs in miniature—to scale, using the same materials as the original—for the price one might pay for an actual chair. Modernist chair lovers collect these and display them as design trophies. As sitting is a basic human need, the chair is the most common of functional objects, and so it's perhaps no surprise that it has evolved into an art form.

Interior designers select all the **furniture** for a space, from hard pieces such as tables, freestanding shelving, credenzas, and cabinets (often called "case goods") to upholstered items such as sofas, beds, and, of course, chairs. When specifying furniture, the goal is to connect the design concept and overall feeling of the space with functionality, comfort, and durability. Designers can look to retail stores, as these often offer ready-made furniture with shorter lead times and options for finishes and fabric selections. For high-end residential projects, designers utilize showrooms that are to-the-trade, meaning only those with a resale certificate can purchase these items for their clients. There are also online retailers that sell straight to consumers, often at lower costs, as well as online auction houses such as 1stdibs, where designers can find coveted vintage pieces. For large-scale projects, designers work with furniture representatives from manufacturers such as Allsteel and Haworth. An example would be for an office project, where customized workstations would be designed from an extensive kit of parts.

Designers also create custom pieces for clients: these require drawings with dimensions and material specifications, which are sent to the manufacturer (woodworker, metalworker, upholsterer, etc.). Shop drawings—highly detailed drawings from the vendor—will then be sent to the designer for approval before the unique piece is created. Sometimes this process will include collaborating with three or four vendors; it takes a lot of work and patience to produce one-of-a-kind designs.

See also FF+E, page 142

Designer   Space Copenhagen
Manufacturer   Fredericia
Product   Swoon Lounge Chair

We've come a long way since 1878, when Thomas Edison created the first electric lightbulb. From incandescent to fluorescent, high-intensity discharge (HID) to light-emitting diode (LED), the array of bulb choices can be overwhelming. While the wattage is the amount of energy used, it is brightness and color, measured on the lumen and Kelvin scales respectively, that makes all the difference to the mood of a space.

Residential, commercial, and institutional spaces all incorporate several **lighting** types; perhaps unsurprisingly, larger projects require a more complex lighting plan. Interior designers align lighting strategies with the concept in the preliminary design phase, since illumination has a large impact on the feeling of a space. On specialty or large projects, designers may work with a lighting designer; either way, designers have a strong understanding of fixture types, lamp options, and switching systems so that they can communicate their vision to the electrical engineer.

The four basic types of lighting—ambient, accent, task, and decorative—are typically present in most projects. Ambient refers to general lighting that brightens an overall space, and includes downlighting, mounted ceiling fixtures, and lighting within a suspended or dropped ceiling (such a grid system is common in office spaces as well as in projects with limited budgets). Accent lighting highlights something noteworthy, such as an artwork, while task lighting is used for a specific function, such as working or reading. Finally, decorative lighting is meant to be a design accessory, such as a good-looking chandelier, sconce, or table light that adds to the overall design of the room. Used together, these lighting types provide both visibility and beauty. Let there be light!

See also Natural Light, page 46, and Daylight, page 174

Designer   Jason Miller
Manufacturer   Roll & Hill
Product   Mini Endless Light

Knickknacks, baubles, tchotchkes, doodads, objets d'art. There may be many names for items that add a finishing touch to an interior, but one thing is clear: adding intentional **accessories** to a space makes an interior feel *livable*. These can be trays, vases, books, candles, mirrors, and other objects that add dimension and visual interest, and tie into the program or the client's personality. Vases filled with flowers speak to biophilia, lit candles bring warmth, and frames filled with photographs bring a personal story to a space. Interiors with character often display many objects meaningful to the inhabitant of the space, such as souvenirs from years of travel, coffee-table books about a favorite topic, or a well-loved ceramics collection.

Designers select accessories that tie into the design concept through the subject, color, texture, or form of the object, to create a balanced composition, visual interest, or a focal point in a room. Often, the repetition of similar items creates a strong visual display; anything, even a very basic object, can become part of a collection, which is often greater than the sum of its parts. Plates displayed en masse on a wall, a grouping of seashells, or art books arranged by color can become an interesting collection that sometimes rivals more expensive art.

While some accessories provide a visual story, others are more functional, such as a clock or a container. While smoking is restricted in most public interiors, ashtrays have always been functional objects with a sculptural quality, such as German designer Marianne Brandt's iconic ashtray from 1924. She designed this while studying at the metal workshop at the Bauhaus, along with many other beautiful yet functional objects of honest material and form—all welcome qualities for an accessory to complete a space.

See also Inspiration, page 58

Designer   Darryl Carter
Project   Private residence
Location   Washington, DC, US

Nineteen-eighties pop artist Keith Haring stated, "Art should be something that liberates your soul, provokes the imagination, and encourages people to go further." A well-designed interior should do the same; in that sense, art and design are inextricably linked. In any form, art enlivens and adds meaning to a space. A well-designed, functional interior that encompasses a creative piece adds a level of curiosity through its subject matter and medium.

The color, line, shape, or form of an **artwork** can inspire a color palette, furniture selection, and overall design concept. The designer may be a part of the art selection process and work directly with an art consultant or gallery to collaborate on pieces that will connect with the interior. Other times, the designer will select from galleries, art shows, auction houses, artists' websites, or thrift shops. Original work is available for all budgets, which makes it easy for designers to introduce a beautiful or provocative piece into an interior, rather than posters or reproductions.

Public spaces that include art—often but not limited to large-scale paintings and sculpture—allow users to view significant and thoughtful pieces outside of a museum. When dealing with the selection of a work, less is often more, allowing each piece in a room to carry a certain weight. In his iconic Glass House, built in 1949, American architect Philip Johnson selected only two artworks, even though he was a voracious collector and one-time curator at the Museum of Modern Art in New York. The painting by Nicolas Poussin titled *Burial of Phocion* from 1648 adds to the focus on nature and connects the color palette of the interior to the exterior, and a sculpture by Elie Nadelman titled *Two Circus Women* from 1930 adds a textural, human quality—both create a division of space in an otherwise open rectangle. With so few pieces, one truly appreciates the importance of each.

See also Art, page 22

Designer   Philip Johnson
Project   The Glass House
Location   New Canaan, CT, US

With new interior walls and openings come doors. And with doors comes **hardware**. And with hardware come a great many decisions.

The selection of hardware sets is dependent on the function of the door: common types include privacy sets for locking doors, passage sets for doors with knobs or levers that turn but don't lock, and dummy knobs for doors that do not turn or lock (these are decorative and often used for closet or cabinets). Then there is specialty hardware, such as flush pulls for pocket doors (doors that slide into the wall). Designers also specify hinges (typically two to four on each door depending on the height and weight of the door); stops (to prevent the door from bumping into the wall when open); catches, often magnetic, that keep the door closed; and different types of locks, such as deadbolts and guards (often used in hotel rooms). Double doors also need flush bolts to keep one leaf stable.

Designers create door and hardware schedules for the contractor, which are spreadsheets that indicate every door in an interior—its location, dimensions, and other features such as door type (solid core, fiberglass, etc.)—as well as all the hardware types and quantities needed for each. Designers also specify decorative hardware for kitchen, bath, and storage cabinetry, where the options are endless (knobs versus levers, cabinet knobs versus pulls, and so on). Levers are easier to grasp for those with arthritis, which is important when specifying for older populations or those who have difficulties grasping a knob.

Hardware comes in varied materials and colors—the most common being chrome, stainless steel, brass, bronze, and black—in finishes such as matte or polished. Designers make their selections based on the client, project type, and overall concept of the space. Hardware is the finishing touch that accentuates the design and adds some sparkle…there is a reason it is referred to as the "jewelry of the home."

See also Metal, page 126, and Kitchen + Bathroom, page 154

Designer   Clodagh
Manufacturer   Du Verre Hardware
Product   Primitive Collection

If included in the scope of the work, interior designers select kitchen and bath appliances, plumbing fixtures and fittings, and even washers and dryers for laundry rooms. For **kitchens**, the designer will determine the basic needs with the client, such as gas or electric, but will specify cooktops based on layout, size, and style and finish to correlate with the design. Cooktops, ovens, hoods, microwaves, refrigerators, warming drawers, and even espresso machines can be built into the cabinetry to work seamlessly with the design. Sink depth, size, shape, and finish, as well as faucet (tap) style (single handle, pull down, or widespread faucet) and finish (stainless steel, chrome, nickel, copper, bronze, gold, or black), are all specified by the designer. Large-scale commercial kitchens in spaces such as dormitories and hospitals require expert kitchen consultants, who sometimes work with the interior designer for overall design cohesion, such as an open kitchen concept in a restaurant.

In **bathrooms**, plumbing fixtures such as the toilet, sink, bathtub, and shower are permanent elements that connect to the water supply, along with faucets and showerheads, while fittings can be moved, such as vanities, towel holders, and toilet paper holders. Even within a shower, there are a range of options such as shower heads, handheld units, wall-mounted jets, and sprays. In large-scale projects, bathrooms need to be accessible and code compliant, while sustainable features that conserve water and energy are becoming more mainstream. Hands-free fixtures that use sensors are the hygienic option, and reduce excess water and soap consumption, with electrical dryers replacing paper towels. Good air quality and ventilation is also a must.

As the bath has become the "spa" of an interior, so its design in projects such as hotels has become the litmus test for good taste. Some well-designed restaurants are famous for their restrooms…even more so than their food!

See also Water Efficiency, page 168, and Accessibility, page 194

Manufacturer   Dornbracht
Product   Tara faucets

White Dove, Cloud White, Simply White, and Super White are just four of the many white paints offered from Benjamin Moore. What is the difference between Simply White and Super White? A lot, according to designers who select **paint** colors and finishes for walls, ceilings, and woodwork (doors, trim, cabinetry).

Paint can transform a space through color, as well as protect interior surfaces against dust, sun, humidity, water, and natural wear. The basic components are pigment (for color), binder (for adhesion), and solvent (for the base). Paints generally fall into two types—water-based and oil-based. Water-based paints are low VOC (volatile organic compounds), which means they include fewer toxic chemicals, but there are also zero-VOC paints and natural paints such as those based on milk, clay, and chalk. With unlimited color choices (including custom mixing) and five main finish options including flat (matte), eggshell, satin, semigloss, and high gloss, no single paint type or finish works for all project types. Oil-based paints have natural or synthetic oil as one of their components, and dry to a hard, resistant finish. However, their production is now being phased out due to their harmful chemical ingredients.

A coat of white paint can make a room feel clean and fresh, while a colorful mural is a wonderful way to bring art into a space. New wall construction is ready for paint; however, existing walls need to be sufficiently prepared so that the surface is clean and smooth. This means that previous paint is scraped and sanded; holes, cracks, and dents are caulked; and dirt and dust are removed. A poorly prepared wall will result in an uneven, messy job, making visible every irregularity.

The decision about where to apply paint and what color depends on the design concept and overall palette. Lighting and quality of surfaces will determine the finish, which will then determine the durability and reflectivity, the maintenance required, and the visibility of surface flaws. Specialty finishes such as faux, sponged, crackled, and metallic are available, which create highly textured and unique looks. The options are endless.

See also Color Theory, page 40, and Color Psychology, page 42

Designer   Design, Bitches
Project   Accomplice
Location   Los Angeles, CA, US

A handful of wallpaper designs have become so iconic that they have come to represent a time and place in history. *Martinique* by CW Stockwell, famously installed at the Beverly Hills Hotel in 1949, incorporates tropical banana leaves and evokes mid-century California luxe; *Hicks' Hexagon* by Cole & Son conjures swinging 1960s London vibes; and *Pimpernel* by Morris & Co. from 1876 lends an Arts and Crafts handmade authenticity.

The wall area, as a significant part of an interior, makes a strong impact on how the user experiences the space. **Wallcoverings**, as in the examples above, add to the design; create a focal point or a backdrop to an interior; and add color, pattern, and texture to a space. Compared with paint, which needs frequent touch-ups, wallpaper, when installed by a professional, has a longer shelf life. Most are easy to wipe down and provide strong sound absorption, which is important in public interiors.

Based on project type, designers select residential or commercial (known as contract) wallcovering; the latter requires more durability and ease of maintenance, and needs to be rated to pass fire inspections for building permits. In the United States, this is indicated as Class A, B, or C, which rates the coverings according to smoke density and flame spread (Class A is strongest at reducing the spread of fire). There is also Type I (light use), Type II (medium use), and Type III (heavy use), which relate to the performance tests for vinyl wallcoverings. The UK and the European Union have similar reaction-to-fire classes. The environmentally conscious may choose PVC-free wallpaper (PVC, or polyvinyl chloride, contains toxic chemicals). Residential or low-traffic projects have even more choices, including natural materials such as paper, bamboo, cork, jute, or grass cloth. Those who say designers merely "pick wallpaper" don't realize how complicated the process can be.

See also Pattern, page 44

Designer   Design, Bitches
Project   Nong La
Location   Los Angeles, CA, US

There is nothing cozier than walking barefoot on a soft **rug**. And, while specifying one may seem like a simple decision, the designer considers myriad aspects before selecting. Color, pattern, material, construction, size, location, usage, durability, maintenance, and budget all factor into the final choice. Since a rug is free-floating and non-permanent, most designers will specify a pad underneath to keep it from shifting. In this, rugs are different from carpet, which often runs from wall-to-wall and is directly adhered to the floor.

Rugs generally fall into two categories, natural or synthetic, although there can be a combination of both. Natural includes wool, cotton, silk, and grass (such as sisal, jute, or bamboo), and animal skins such as leather or sheepskin. Synthetic includes microfiber, polyester, rayon, and polypropylene. The material is significant as it changes the feel of a rug, as well as the durability and the budget. Silk rugs are the gold standard in luxury, while wool rugs are extremely durable; a polyester rug is the least expensive but does not wear as well.

Like furniture, rugs are sold at a variety of retailers, from online to to-the-trade, such as STARK, which operates high-end showrooms in design centers in major cities such as New York, Chicago, and London. Rug companies also collaborate with interior designers to create new products, such as Sasha Bikoff X Rug Art, a collection of concentric circles, ovals, and squares in multiple colorways. Vintage rugs are used in projects to tell a story; Oriental, Turkish, and Persian rugs have remained iconic for their exquisite patterns and colors that embody cross-cultural and global appeal. All it takes is an online search at ABC Carpet & Home, the New York-based rug emporium, to see the sheer variety of options and realize that rugs really are art for the floor.

See also Textiles, page 136

Designer   Sasha Bikoff Interior Design
Project   Private residence
Location   Bridgehampton, NY, US

8.0 —— Environmetal

While there are many different **certification** programs, standards, and
systems with varying criteria and philosophies for buildings and interiors,
all strive to be more thoughtful about how the demolition, design, renovation,
and construction processes—as well as the structures' consumption of
water, energy, raw materials, and other resources—impact the environment.
Rating systems such as Leadership in Energy and Environmental Design
(LEED) and the Building Research Establishment Environmental Assessment
Methodology (BREEAM) were developed to increase transparency, provide
clearly defined strategies that are measurable, and create visible outcomes.
Operating and maintaining the structure, for example, cannot be an
afterthought: it must be considered at the initial phase of a project. Some
certifications also focus on the health and well-being of the inhabitants and
users of these structures, since people spend nearly all their time indoors.
Requirements such as minimizing pollutants and demanding acoustic
comfort should not be viewed as excessive or remarkable.

     To obtain certification for a space (such as LEED for Interior Design
and Construction) or building, metrics established as either performance
requirements or goals to satisfy must be achieved to earn points or credits.
There may be varying degrees or levels of compliance that can be acquired
within the rating system; this would be determined by evaluating what
objectives are achievable and if the criteria for attaining those goals meet
the stakeholders' intentions.

     Certification isn't only good for the environment and for users; over
time, the initial, up-front costs of making buildings compliant are likely to
be recuperated, and during the life of the project the savings will add up.
Some incentives for investing in more sustainable, healthier environments
can include reduced operating and maintenance costs and an increase in
the property's value. The demand for healthier spaces and buildings should
not be ignored.

See also Comfort, page 180

Designer   Henry J Lyons
Project   Central Bank of Ireland
Location   Dublin, Ireland

It is the case that for nearly all **materials** specified and installed inside a space, the interior designer does not generally know how or where the raw components were obtained, what ingredients were used, and how an item was manufactured. Even though today's world is interconnected, there is a detachment between the people who make or obtain goods and the people who specify or use them, similar to the way that most food produce travels from far-flung parts of the globe before landing on diners' plates.

To shed some light on this very opaque supply chain, manufacturers of materials that, for example, are sustainably harvested or produced, have a positive impact on the environment, or support healthier indoor air quality have the option to disclose and identify the sources of the contents, as well as other factors such as emissions and consumption of water and energy during production. An independent third party overseeing the verification of these and other disclosures creates confidence that the claims made by the producer are valid and holds them accountable, providing assurance for all parties involved. This level of transparency communicates that the company is not only committed to a healthier environment but that the information it is reporting is, in fact, accurate and correctly demonstrates the product's sustainable attributes.

To make informed decisions, the interior designer must take the time to research the materials they want to use as well as the maintenance procedures required for a given item once installed, as this can minimize the number of harmful pollutants people are exposed to daily. Expanding awareness of hazards and holding manufacturers accountable is an ongoing process but, ultimately, this examination is under the purview of the interior designer. With time, advocacy will promote and encourage more demand for safer products and finishes .

See also Specifications, page 198

Water is a precious resource that cannot be taken for granted. Consider the absolute necessity of its consumption for the survival of all living beings, as well as its use to ensure physical hygiene and many other uses for daily tasks: in short, sustaining life on Earth is not possible without it. For most in the developed world, turning on the faucet and expecting clean water is a given—until it's not available or is contaminated. Yet scarcity of clean water is a recurring problem in many parts of the world; even in areas where it's readily available, its quality may sometimes be compromised, thus imparting deep distrust in the ongoing safety of the water and in the municipality providing it. Water's value cannot be overstated, and rethinking how its waste is minimized begins with challenging the perception that there is an endless supply of it.

     Methods for water conservation vary in their complexity, costs, and necessity for collaboration with consultants. Interior designers are aware of different approaches, and because a substantial amount of water use occurs indoors it is essential to impart some knowledge to end users. By specifying items such as faucets with sensors, toilets that use less water to flush, water-saving shower heads, and waterless urinals, water use will automatically decrease. Challenging the status quo of how water is "typically" used or spent needs to be examined by all who contribute to the built environment: drinkable water must not be diverted for anything—such as the operation of mechanical systems—other than human consumption. Gray water (water collected after dishes and hands have been washed) should be available to flush toilets; storm water, rather than flowing into the sewers, along with rainwater from roofs, can be captured and stored for future irrigation. **Water efficiency** begins with the interior designer's specifications and their efforts to persuade the client to see it as something of value, rather than allowing it to literally flow down the drain.

See also Kitchen + Bathroom, page 154

Designer   //3877 + KNEAD HD
Project   Mi Vida Wharf
Location   Washington, DC, US

Can indoor spaces make people sick? What chemical pollutants are in the materials of the treatments and furnishings in a room? It's common to find volatile organic compound (VOC) levels higher indoors than out, since they are present in items such as carpeting, paints, composite wood products (for example, kitchen cabinets), and furniture. Exposure to too many VOCs can cause people to experience throat, nose, and eye irritation; headaches; and nausea. Prolonged contact damages the kidneys, liver, and nervous system.

It might be assumed that poor **indoor air quality** can be resolved simply by opening a window, but getting—and keeping—fresh air inside a room is not always that easy. In some spaces, particularly office buildings, windows are not even operable. Systems to exchange, circulate and filter the air can remove any buildup of CO_2 and particulate matter that is brought in from outside, as well as some pollutant VOCs and other gases. This, and how the building "breathes," is the purview of the mechanical engineer, although some home air filters are also available.

But perhaps the best way to ensure good indoor air quality is to seek materials that do not emit harmful substances in the first place: these include stone, glass, wood, porcelain and ceramic tiles, and metals. The designer's awareness and knowledge of these and other hazards in the objects and furnishings that surround people plays a significant role in the reduction of such toxins in indoor spaces. Coordination with the mechanical engineer to provide more than the baseline circulation of air is absolutely essential. Trying to keep a space toxin-free should never be an afterthought, as the use of non-toxic materials is beneficial not only for the welfare of its inhabitants and users but for all involved in the fabrication, procurement, installation, and maintenance of materials.

See also Heating, Ventilation + Air Conditioning, page 188

With most of the world still reliant on fossil fuels to heat and cool the inside of buildings, it is not surprising that structures consume significant and vast amounts of natural resources to keep inhabitants comfortable. Unfortunately, this comfort comes by way of depleting those materials that are limited in quantity or being used at a rate that far outstrips demand. Not only are CO_2 emissions high owing to the expenditure of these resources, thus contributing to warmer global temperatures, but the processes used to extract them are extremely detrimental to the environment. Our dependence on these resources is unsustainable: alternatives exist to answer the need to provide light, power equipment, and create thermally comfortable interiors, but their use must be radically increased.

Some strategies that interior designers use to create an **energy-efficient** space are straightforward and are typically economical, such as specifying window treatments to shade spaces. Harnessing daylight is one of the most effective ways to illuminate areas (although too much can heat the space, thus requiring mitigation—preferably not through energy-hungry air conditioning), while installing occupancy sensors that automatically turn off lighting when the system does not detect movement is very practical. Setting lighting to timers can also mitigate the use of power, as this also avoids lights being on long after the workday is over, which contributes to light pollution as well as energy wastage. Use energy-efficient lighting to light spaces, such as LEDs (light-emitting diodes), which do not heat up, thus requiring less demand on the HVAC (heating, ventilation, and air conditioning) system. Because they are long-lasting, they need to be replaced less frequently than other lamps (bulbs), which offsets their higher initial cost and saves money in the long term. Interior designers also specify equipment and appliances that meet energy-efficiency standards, verified through a third party.

Other approaches are situational, such as the availability of solar power, access to natural ventilation, and the glass or glazing used for the building (such as low emissivity or "low-e," which is glass that has a special coating applied to minimize heat gain during the summer and heat loss during the winter).

See also Lighting, page 146

It is possible to rise early in the morning while it is still dark outside, go to a windowless office, eat lunch at one's desk, and leave at the end of the workday after the last of the sun's rays slip below the horizon for the evening. For many, this is an all-too-common scenario. But not seeing natural light throughout the day can have detrimental effects, including low productivity, lethargy, and the inability to manage stress.

Views of nature, observing the seasons as well as the passing of time during the day, has a positive influence on people's sleep–wake cycles, thus affecting mood and attentiveness. Even the management of pain can be affected by a patient's exposure to sunlight: those who recover in shady rooms have reported greater amounts of discomfort, requiring more medicine to manage pain, than those whose rooms have brighter natural light. All this information is supported by research, and making design decisions grounded in this analysis for positive results for people is the foundation of evidence-based design (EBD), which is most frequently applied to healthcare facilities, but can be used for any other interiors.

It is important to design so that the level of lighting for visual acuity is paramount, but, typically, meeting that minimum criterion is achieved through specifying artificial light. Bringing **daylight** into spaces supports a quality of light that is essential to the physical and mental well-being of the inhabitants and users. There can be, however, too much of a good thing: With excessive or unintended exposure to sunlight, glare and increased heat gain must be recognized as potential problems. However, through the use of shading devices, visual comfort and lower heat gain can be attained.

See also Natural Light, page 46

Humans have an innate desire to **connect to nature**. In fact, spending time outdoors can positively impact one's emotional and mental state. Unfortunately, it's not always feasible to spend time amid nature, especially in densely populated cities where greenery is nearly nonexistent. Depending on the place where one works—such as a warehouse, factory, or office that has no access to windows—even seeing the outdoors may not be possible. Such deprivation may be compounded by much of the built environment, which is barren and devoid of the stimuli that are found in nature, such as water, vegetation, natural ventilation, and sunlight.

As modern people, we may be widely assumed to have no urgency or desire to relate with the natural world, but the unwitting consequences of this detachment may result in stress, anxiety, fatigue, and overall impaired health. When people are provided with the opportunity to have physical access to gardens or water, either within interior spaces or outside, their inherent love of nature, or biophilia, is aroused, leading to improved well-being for adults and children.

Nature-enriched environments foster a greater sense of connection to a particular place, because of one's ability to observe beauty and experience feelings of satisfaction. Witnessing the gradual changes in the seasons reminds the viewer of the cyclical existence of all things on Earth. It only makes sense, therefore, that designers create interiors that respond to this innate desire; by providing nourishing spaces that delight the senses, they feed people's instinctive need to see and be a part of the natural world.

See also Biophilia, page 48

8.7 ⎯ Environmental

Designer   Bestor Architecture
Project   Private residence
Location   Los Angeles, CA, US

There exists an intricate relationship between **mind and body**; tending to only physical ailments does not necessarily address the underlying causes that may be connected to one's mental state. Interior design can provide spaces that allow the nourishment of both, but appropriate approaches must be considered at the early stages of a project.

Providing views to nature and sunlight is one way of directly contributing to people's well-being. More overt approaches include assisting clients by discussing and identifying particular needs that employees might have for a supportive environment. When consensus has been established around designing dedicated spaces in the workplace to support restorative activities—such as meditation or prayer rooms, yoga studios, exercise rooms, and even nap areas—it demonstrates that the employer is serious about the contentment and health of those who work there.

Standing while working at a computer might appear to be a strange novelty, but the ability to have that choice is important as prolonged hours of being seated can cause health issues. Interior designers can cater to such needs, and can also encourage movement through the arrangement of spaces, such as placing printers in a zone away from where everyone is working. Designing levels in such a way that users are encouraged to use the staircase between floors, rather than taking the elevator, helps mitigate issues such as high blood pressure, unhealthy cholesterol levels, and obesity.

When interior designers provide additional spaces such as bike storage and shower areas, it communicates to the staff that the workplace encourages activity through alternative means of transportation, thus valuing their physical fitness (not to mention the saving of CO_2 emissions).

While all of these might be seen as extras or perks, consider the benefits of healthy and happy people—what employer wouldn't want to encourage that?

See also Sensory Balance, page 50

Designer   Clodagh
Project   Miraval Spa Berkshires
Location   Lenox, MA, US

Being either too hot or too cold is not uncommon for some—especially in the workplace, where individuals usually cannot manage the thermostat. Yes, fans, space heaters, and one sweater more or less can ease the discomfort of being thermally uncomfortable, but is it possible to exercise greater control over the interior environment?

Achieving the optimal temperature for everyone is, admittedly, nearly impossible, given the fact that it is highly subjective and even throughout the day a person's level of **comfort** can fluctuate. One strategy that interior designers use is to consider zones rather than treating the space as a monolithic area that is all heated or cooled to the same degree, regardless of the various functions, equipment, or occupant density within any given location. This approach is also insensitive to the orientation of the building in relation to the sun's path, which can greatly impact the amount of heat gained. Conversely, with different zones, greater control of the thermostat is possible and temperatures can vary between the zones.

Acoustic comfort can also be an issue, given several external sources and factors that one does not often consider, such as traffic, proximity to industrial sites, and transportation (noise from trains and planes is extremely disruptive). Inside, if people are constantly unsettled by surrounding conversations in an open office environment, this can lead to high levels of dissatisfaction. In a busy restaurant, hard surfaces, such as wood or ceramic tile floors, along with ceilings made of drywall (plasterboard) and very few soft or upholstered areas, turn a conversation into an unpleasant activity. Even ducts and other HVAC equipment can vibrate, creating unwanted background noise that is only perceived when the system shuts off temporarily.

It is critical for interior designers to consider these issues at the outset of a project so that users are not exposed to a constant barrage of noise, as an excessive amount can hinder sleep, affect the ability to focus, and inhibit productivity.

See also Sensory Balance, page 50, and Heating, Ventilation + Air Conditioning, page 188

Designer   Bates Masi + Architects
Project   Private residence
Location   Amagansett, NY, US

Through research, it has been proven that the interior environment can greatly impact one's mental health, whether positively or negatively. People who view their dwelling as messy are prone to be tired and depressed, rather than perceiving it as a place to relax. Controlling the amount of clutter that surrounds a person often correlates directly to mood, anxiety, and even confidence. Deciding what to remove and what remains reinforces a sense of self-efficacy, or recognition of one's competence to make a plan and execute it.

Seeing and experiencing disorder can overwhelm a person's sense of composure, as well as hinder the ability to find a particular item at a moment's notice or gain a sense of orientation. Continually looking for items on a recurring basis can frustrate a person, and fuel the sense of being scattered rather than being focused, calm, and in control. Through **order**, a sense of serenity infuses a space and, by extension, the people who live or work in it.

With the acquisition of personal possessions and the constant accumulation of things—look no further than the proliferation of storage units that hold the overflow of such material clutter—it is understandable that the public is eager to find guidance in ways to structure and declutter their spaces. Marie Kondo, the Japanese organizing consultant, has found massive popularity through her books, the first one of which, *The Life-Changing Magic of Tidying Up*, sold more than 13 million copies worldwide. New York-based professional organizer Laura Cattano notes that introspection is of the utmost importance, since "the first step of organizing has nothing to do with stuff," but rather, "it's about clarifying who you are and how you want to live." It is very evident that there is a massive appetite for creating a sense of refuge or retreat, especially regarding one's home, to support well-being.

See also Harmony, page 32

Designer   Neri&Hu
Project   The Urban Oasis at Alila Bangsar
Location   Kuala Lumpur, Malaysia

9.0 —— Technical

The public's most common perception of the interior designer's work is that its scope is limited to the selection and specification of materials and products. While that is a portion of the responsibilities, the United States-based National Council for Interior Design Qualification states that the designer who successfully completes the NCIDQ exam has "proven their expertise in understanding and applying current **codes** [or regulations] established to protect public health, safety, and welfare."

Exiting a doctor's office in a high-rise building without harm is not given a second thought, until there is smoke choking the corridors and the way one entered is no longer accessible. Elevators are not functioning and even more dangerous is the crowd of panicked people adding to the confusion. This describes an extreme situation, but knowledge of the codes and adherence to them is a reason why the discipline requires education, especially for commercial interiors. In the example above, interior designers must know a simple thing like which direction a door swings open, as the wrong way can impair a person's ability to exit a space.

Historically, codes were established as a means of keeping the builder honest. The Code of Hammurabi, a Babylonian legal text written in the 18th century BCE, states, "If a builder builds a house for a man and does not make its construction firm, and the house which he has built collapses and causes the death of the owner of the house, that builder shall be put to death." Unfortunately, it has often taken tragedies and loss of life to be the impetus for developing codes, such as the Great Chicago Fire of 1871, which devastated almost 3½ square miles (9 square kilometres) of the city and killed an estimated 300 people. For this reason, governments and local jurisdictions adopt codes as measures to keep the public safe in the built environment. Codes encompass all facets of building construction, including architecture, interior design, structural, mechanical, electrical, and plumbing.

See also Process Part II, page 222

Designer //3877 + KNEAD HD
Project Mi Vida District Wharf
Location Washington, DC, US

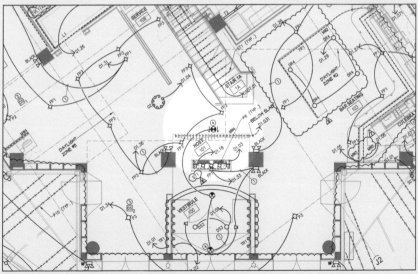

Being comfortable indoors is something that many take for granted. Bringing warm or cooled air into a built environment, no matter the temperature outside, has enabled people to inhabit more extreme climates. **Heating**, **ventilation**, **and air conditioning** (HVAC) systems must be designed by mechanical engineers, but coordination with the designer is required to establish how they connect and appear within the interiors.

In more upscale areas, such as a lobby or a conference room, large diffusers are visually distracting in the ceiling. By engaging with the interior designer to understand their vision or intent, the mechanical engineer can identify alternative locations as well as specify different diffusers, while maintaining the necessary flow and exchange of air. Providing enough space above the finished ceiling, known as the plenum space, is required, since ducts, piping, and electrical wiring inhabit this area and, in some locations, must be accessible. A drywall (plasterboard) ceiling, while aesthetically pleasing, must have access panels in discreet areas so that the equipment can be reached. An exposed ceiling, which creates visual interest, can be challenging, as what is normally hidden will be visible and will therefore require careful placement and attention to installation—it must be tidy so as to not call attention to any particular object; a typical strategy is to paint everything one color.

While interior designers do not design the systems that permit proper airflow, they approve the system locations, exposed duct and vent styles, and finishes. They are aware of the detrimental side effects that can compromise the comfort and health of the occupants if these aspects are not considered. Working with the mechanical engineer, interior designers understand the strategies of how good indoor air quality can be established, and work toward educating the client.

See also Indoor Air Quality, page 170

Designer   //3877 + KNEAD HD
Project   Mi Vida 14th Street
Location   Washington, DC, US

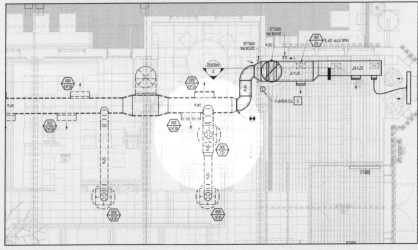

The oversight of the interior designer includes identifying locations of outlets, knowing their types (a duplex, quad, dedicated, or ground fault circuit interrupter), and coordinating the locations with equipment or anything that needs **electrical** power. In addition, designers specify and locate lighting, and establish switch locations within spaces: all of this must be included in the construction drawings. This typically requires coordination with the client and consultants to understand what is necessary, where power is needed, and the equipment's electrical requirements.

For example, for a cluster of workstations, the designer might specify that the power be provided from below and through the concrete slab, requiring it to be drilled so that the wiring can be pulled through the hole and connected to the workstation panels. This information is received by the electrical engineer, who produces their own set of documents. The designer must prepare drawings identifying locations for power and a lighting schedule (a list of every light fixture with details about the manufacturer, voltage, output, and other information), along with a reflected ceiling plan (which shows ceiling features as if they were reflected on to the floor below), positioning each luminaire.

Comprehending how the electrical power and wiring is distributed within a space is the purview of the electrical engineer. While they are typically not lighting designers, they have knowledge of lighting control systems, and can produce energy and lighting calculations. The drawings they contribute pertain to powering the space and equipment (such as outlets and sources that provide electricity) and assigning circuitry for lighting. Additional drawings and information that may not be so obvious include fire alarm locations, emergency lighting, and panel board schedules (a diagram or table instructing the electrician how and what wiring connects the equipment or lighting back to the power panel; it also includes the various electrical load requirements for every item). Prior to completing the construction of ceilings and walls, inspections must be carried out to check that the wiring has been properly installed

See also Lighting, page 146, and Coordination, page 204

Designer   //3877 + KNEAD HD
Project   The Grill
Location   Washington, DC, US

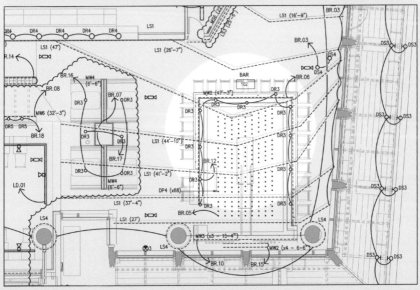

The interior designer provides layouts of bathrooms, pantries, and kitchens, and specifies items such as toilets, sinks, faucets (taps), and showers; if they are working on a restaurant, for example, a commercial kitchen consultant will typically be brought in early in the process. All of this requires coordination with a **plumbing** engineer, whose responsibilities include designing the system that provides water, managing the wastewater and venting, and considering factors such as water pressure and distribution— all to meet the demands of the occupants. Some mechanical equipment that heats and cools spaces also requires the expertise of the plumbing engineer. Water-heating equipment is under their purview, as is its distribution and its availability in a timely manner. For wastewater and drainage, the plumbing engineer must consider pipe sizes so they permit proper flow, as well as the pipes' slopes as they must connect to the sewer system or septic tanks. This must be coordinated with other systems, such as mechanical ducts, to avoid conflicts within the space above the ceiling.

Interior designers specify various fixtures to conserve water, such as dual-flush toilets, high-efficiency toilets (HETs) that use only about 1⅓ gallons (5 litres) per flush, rather than the typical 1⅗ gallons (6 litres), waterless urinals (gravity works to drain the waste while oil above it keeps odors from rising), touchless faucets, and water-saving shower heads. More ambitious methods of water conservation, such as harvesting rainwater or reusing water captured from sinks, basins, and washing machines—known as gray water—to flush toilets, require the coordination and expertise of a plumbing engineer.

See also Kitchen + Bathroom, page 154, and Water Efficiency, page 168

Designer //3877 + KNEAD HD
Project   The Grill
Location Washington, DC, US

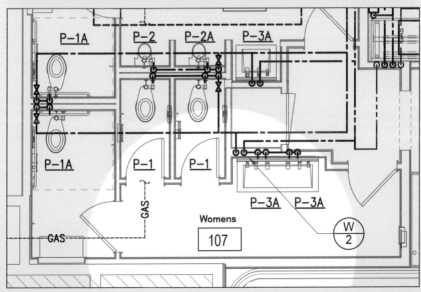

While people without disabilities walk up and down stairs or move through passageways that are narrow or obstructed without a second thought, nearly 16 percent of the world's population is excluded from these seemingly simple activities. According to the World Health Organization, about one in six people have a visual or mobility impairment. To address concerns arising from this, interior designers must consider the entire population and the diverse conditions that define humans: this is accomplished by creating spaces that are **accessible**. After all, if people are not taken into consideration when designing, what is the purpose? The interior designer's goal is to create interiors where function, accessibility, and aesthetics combine to contribute a feeling of safety and a sense of enjoyment for all occupants.

      In the United States, the prevailing federal civil rights law that is followed is the Americans with Disabilities Act, or ADA (in the EU, there is the European Accessibility Act of 2019). The section of the ADA that pertains most to interior designers states the minimum requirements for the built environment, such as widths of corridors and doorways, adequate maneuvering spaces, heights of countertops, and sinks at appropriate levels for accessibility. These wide-ranging standards address a person's mobility, dexterity, and ability to take in sensory information (predominantly via hearing or sight) within the built environment. For example, when considering a blind person's use of a cane, the interior designer must be sensitive to objects that protrude a certain distance away from the surface of the wall, so that they avoid contact with them. Interior designers must examine the use of ramps (this excludes stairs that separate the floors of a building) for individuals with limited mobility to navigate stairs or any level changes. Indeed, at all times, designers must approach their work with empathy and provide accessibility for everyone.

See also Anthropometrics, page 34

Designer   //3877 + KNEAD HD
Project   The Grill
Location   Washington, DC, US

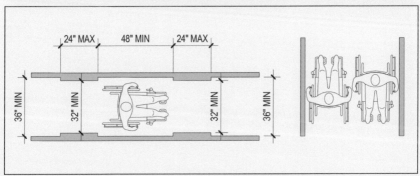

Before a vision is built and becomes reality, there is a high probability that it was conceived as a sketch. The word connotes something that is not quite finished and certainly not in its final form. As the ideas develop from bubble diagrams or test fits into floor plans, these drawings require the designer to generate a closer study of the walls, ceilings, and every other built portion of the project—especially when two or more materials "meet" or transition from one surface or orientation to another. This requires attention to the materials the designer is specifying. How does a wood floor transition to carpet? What is the detail in the ceiling between drywall and an acoustic tile, located at different heights? What is the repeat pattern of a fabric and how is it centered or placed on the back of a custom chair? How large are the wood panel seams on a wall and do they align with other reveals?

Frequently, within the drawing set, **detail drawings** are found after the floor plans, elevations, and sections. Executed at a much larger scale than any other drawings, to see particular aspects and convey the information clearly with notes and dimensions, these require a strong grasp of construction and "how-to" knowledge. Omitting fine awareness of the details in a set of drawings will undoubtedly lead to multiple requests for information (RFI) from the contractor, as well as to changes in orders, which would raise the overall construction costs. A quote attributed to American designers Charles and Ray Eames sums up the importance of this aspect of design and construction: "The details are not details. They make the design."

See also Process Part II, page 222

Designer //3877 + KNEAD HD
Project Mi Vida District Wharf
Location Washington, DC, US

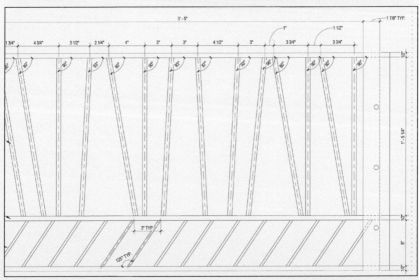

In the design industry, **specifications** can refer to a document that is a part of the construction drawings, which provides written descriptions of the work along with the caliber or quality of workmanship that is required. The scope of labor, as well as which materials are necessary, is recorded in great detail; this information goes beyond the aesthetics or how the space should appear, as executing the construction of a project demands specificity to avoid confusion or errors and provide accuracy. This documentation conveys the designer's explicit intentions and can be referred to when there are discrepancies between what was intended and what was executed or built.

"Specifications" (or "specs") is also the term for the numerous items that the interior designer has selected for a project. Doors identified on a plan must be accounted for regarding their size, thickness, and material, but also their respective hardware set. Every space or room must have finishes identified for the floors, walls, and ceilings. Equipment, lighting, laminates or solid surfaces for millwork or cabinetry, decorative hardware, textiles, furniture, plumbing fixtures, and accessories—any item for all these categories must be identified on the drawings, typically as a spreadsheet, and additionally in floor plans, elevations, sections, and detail drawings. Some of this information is shared with other consultants, such as equipment and lighting selections.

Nearly every item has an associated "cut sheet," which provides a vast amount of detail, often gleaned from the manufacturer's website. This might include maintenance guidance, or what colors or finishes a particular item comes in, as well as dimensions; it is the responsibility of the interior designer to decide and identify all the various aspects, so that nothing is left to question. Amassing all the cut sheets and organizing them into one document or binder for quick and easy reference is paramount for a well-coordinated designer.

See also Materials, page 166, Process Part II, page 222

While interior designers communicate their design intent via the construction drawing set, for some aspects of the project, such as custom work, this document is not actually what subcontractors or people in a particular trade use in order to execute and install a component. For example, the cabinetry, or millwork, is not constructed with prefabricated or ready-made pieces: widths, depths, finishes (such as wood veneer or laminate), thicknesses, substrates (for example, medium-density fiberboard), hinges, and "pulls" (or handles) are all specified by the interior designer. This information— shown in plans, elevations, and sections—is provided to the millworker (joiner), who is responsible for producing **shop drawings**. These documents contain information that allow the components to be fabricated from dimensions that were taken on-site, so that when the millwork is installed it will fit and function exactly as designed.

Shop drawings are then submitted to the interior designer, who must review them in a timely manner, as construction of the millwork will not begin without their approval. Most often, the designer makes notes directly on the shop drawings, communicating minor edits and verifying what is drawn. These are returned to the millworker as approved with edits, or rejected. If the latter occurs, the millworker must resubmit the drawings, but in this situation, it's best to speak directly with them, along with the general contractor, to understand why this is occurring. Delaying the return of any shop drawings will most likely have a detrimental impact on the project's timeline, with knock-on financial repercussions, so timely resolution of any errors and omissions is essential.

See also Drawings, page 92

Designer //3877 + KNEAD HD
Project Mi Vida 14th Street
Location Washington, DC, US

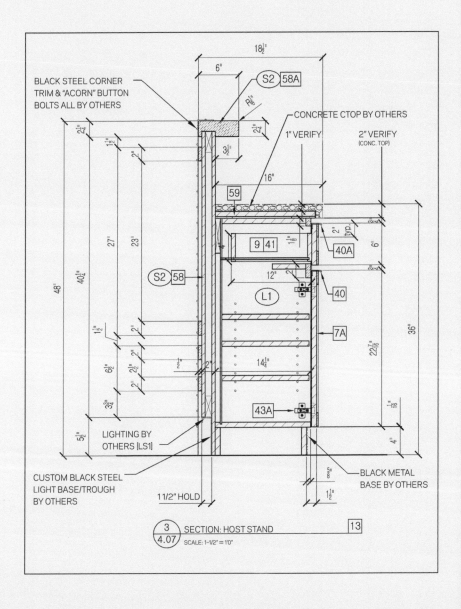

BLACK STEEL CORNER
TRIM & "ACORN" BUTTON
BOLTS ALL BY OTHERS

CONCRETE CTOP BY OTHERS

CUSTOM BLACK STEEL
LIGHT BASE/TROUGH
BY OTHERS

LIGHTING BY
OTHERS [LS1]

BLACK METAL
BASE BY OTHERS

SECTION: HOST STAND
SCALE: 1–1/2" = 1'0"

After the design has been completed and approved and drawings distributed, and the contractor is on board, what is next? Taking the design from drawings to reality is where the rubber meets the road, as the saying goes. Recurring on-site meetings, held with all stakeholders present, assess the progress being made to build the project on time and on budget, during the phase known as **construction administration**, or CA. The designer must work in harmony with the general contractor—in commercial projects, this is the superintendent on-site, as well as the project manager—to answer any questions, provide clarification on the drawings, and develop solutions when the course of action does not go as planned.

No matter how carefully and diligently the drawings are executed, errors and omissions occur—many with financial consequences. If demolition is required on the site to clear the way for new construction, there can be unforeseen problems that must be addressed immediately to keep the project on schedule (and by extension, on budget). Typically documented as requests for information, or RFIs, the contractor sends these to the interior designer for responses that may or may not require a site visit to inspect the problem. A change order—a modification in the contractor's scope of work in the original contract—may need to be written, carefully noting the additional or reduced work and the costs associated with it. For both RFIs and change orders, it is routine for the designer to generate drawings to clarify and document the amended portions of the project.

The designer's thrill is seeing drawings come to life; this takes a while, as the site may start as nothing more than bare concrete, with exposed ducts, pipes, and columns. Slowly, as the space literally begins to take shape, the vision becomes a reality.

See also Process Part II, page 222

Designer   //3877 + KNEAD HD
Project   Mi Vida 14th Street
Location   Washington, DC, US

All who contribute to an interior design project—such as architects, engineers, subcontractors, and consultants—must labor collectively for it to become a reality. No single entity works on a design alone, and this is true for even the smallest undertaking. The responsibility of **coordination** prior to the construction rests mostly with the interior designer. This would include nearly every facet of the process—from ensuring that the drawings and design intent are conveyed to the MEP (mechanical, electrical, plumbing) engineers and providing any important documents, such as lighting cut sheets, to verifying that a fabric selected for a particular piece of furniture is durable and appropriate for the intended use. Every consultant or individual who shares their expertise for the design and execution of the project must be in contact with the interior designer, who is responsible for accurately including the relevant information on the drawings.

After the drawings have been completed and construction begins, the coordination shifts more to the contractor, who must bring subcontractors and tradespeople on to the site in a specific and orderly procedure, as well as all materials, and must see to the removal of debris without too much disruption and untidiness. Additionally, inspections by the local building authorities need to be scheduled in a timely manner. Coordination occurs during weekly construction administration, or CA, meetings, held at the job site, as unforeseen situations can occur. In such instances, the contractor must confer with the interior designer to ensure that a timely resolution is provided. The client is informed of these situations, especially those that impact the budget or the date of completion. Regardless of what occurs, ensuring alignment of all activities depends on constant and clear communication between the myriad parties involved.

See also Process Part II, page 222

Designer   //3877 + KNEAD HD
Project   The Grill
Location   Washington, DC, US

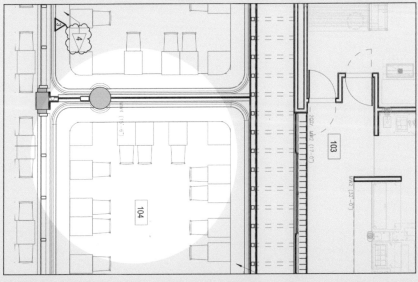

10.0 —— Profession

Ask a designer about their educational experience, and you will often hear the term "**studio culture**." This is a unique learning environment where the core courses of the curriculum are studio-based, meaning there is an emphasis on creative inquiry within a learn-by-doing approach. With more hours than a typical course, studios are usually capped at 16 students per instructor and meet for four or more hours a few days a week, allowing ample time for exploration and experimentation. The studio is constantly abuzz, as students work on projects alongside their classmates, exchanging ideas, peer reviewing, and meeting one-on-one with their professor for desk crits (critiques).

The strongest ideas can come from brainstorming, connecting, and collaborating with other designers, and the studio allows for this natural flow of creativity. Physically, the studios incorporate plenty of workspace to spread out large-format drawings, with oversize desks and ample storage areas for materials, supplies, and works-in-progress (sketches, models, etc.). There is also room and provision for technology, including abundant power sources. Throughout the design process, students receive feedback from peers, faculty, and invited professionals during informal and formal discussions, critiques, and presentations. With pin-up space lining the walls for printed materials, and projectors or large-screen TVs for digital work, students learn to communicate their ideas—both graphically and orally— during all the phases of a project.

Throughout the studio sequence, complexity increases from one semester to the next as projects grow in scale and scope. Students frequently also spend extended hours in the studio, long after class sessions end, continuing to push themselves creatively while creating a bond with their cohort that lasts long after they graduate.

See also Design Thinking, page 68

Along with the core design studio, during their **education** interior design students take supporting studios as well as lecture courses in a variety of topics such as history, sustainability, building systems, and professional practice.

A supporting studio, such as sketching, follows a similar work-in-class approach as the core studios, but is more of a tool to support the work in the core studio. Courses in graphics and digital drafting also support the core studio, as students learn different methods with which to express and communicate their design ideas. Other classes on topics such as materiality, color theory, lighting, and acoustics can be more lecture-oriented; however, most of the curriculum in design school aims for an outcome of original creative work.

Many programs incorporate a lockstep curriculum, meaning students move with their cohort in sequence from one semester to the next. This works with a content-heavy major such as interior design, where students acquire creative and critical thinking skills as well as a range of design-related tools needed for internships and future employment. Along with academic studies, design programs often have strong community-centered activities and events such as student groups, distinguished lecturers, design challenges, and pro-bono projects that serve local neighborhoods.

While the outcome is similar, the actual degree can vary within programs—from a Bachelor of Arts or a Bachelor of Fine Arts, both in interior design, to a Bachelor of Interior Design. The degree type is dependent on requirements that are often regulated, assessed, and accredited by bodies such as the Council of Interior Design Accreditation (CIDA) or the National Association of Schools of Arts and Design (NASAD), both in the United States. Site visitors will evaluate the programs' compliance on a regulated schedule, and review students' work to determine if it reaches standards set by CIDA or NASAD. Programs that are compliant set and maintain a high bar for arts and design education.

See also Critique, page 72

Akin to an audition for a performer, the **portfolio** gives a first look at the capabilities of a designer. Necessary to land an internship, scholarship, teaching gig, or full-time employment, it is a visual representation of a designer's work. Students might create strong projects in school, but they also need to know how to edit and present their work in a clear, compelling way. For the portfolio, students and professionals select the most successful aspects of their school or work projects to show a variety of mediums (hand sketching, digital drafting, three-dimensional renderings, etc.) and projects (small, medium, large, residential, commercial, institutional) to give the reviewer a look inside their creative mind. Designers want to tell a story, and so incorporating process work (sketches, reiterations, study models) gives the project depth and shows how a particular design got from A to B.

Interior designers understand the basic principles of graphic design and often utilize Adobe software—which includes Photoshop, Illustrator, and InDesign—when creating their portfolio. The strongest portfolios are often the least "designed," with minimal text or graphics, so that the work itself stands out. Designers also comprehend best practices in photography, using appropriate lighting and background to show their three-dimensional work.

Often, designers initially send a one- or two-page sample of their work, which gives the reviewer a snapshot of their design philosophy and capabilities, with the hope that the prospective employer wants to see more. Résumés are also important, as they provide detailed information about the job seeker's education, activities, and skills; they should be simple in graphic quality while connecting visually to their portfolio.

Ultimately, designers create a full graphic package that represents their talent and hard work. And, since the portfolio is often sent digitally to a firm or employer, it really needs to "speak" for the designer.

See also Drawings, page 92

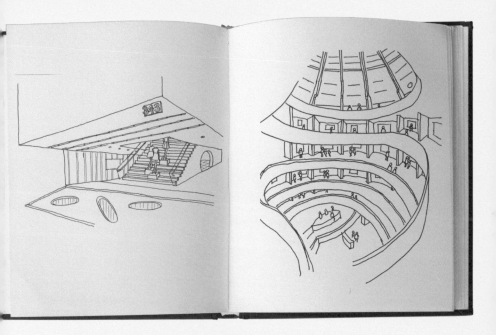

A good **internship** requires a baseline level of skills and some creative acumen, since a design intern will be responsible for far more than just fetching coffee for upper-level designers! In fact, the internship is considered an extended studio in design school, so much so that many design programs either require one for the degree or give college credit to those who complete one. Either way, it is essential for preparing interior designers for the profession, so that they can snag their top job.

While design school tends to emphasize conceptual thinking and process, an internship gets into the nitty-gritty of a project, such as construction drawings, purchase orders, and redlines (drawings with corrections marked up in red)—important elements needed for a project to get built. That is why this initial work exposure is priceless: it gives the student a real view into the profession. Larger firms have internship programs that recruit students across many schools and locations, and include special activities for their interns. Smaller firms will often match the student with a mentor, whom they will assist in various phases of a project. There are also opportunities to "shadow" a designer in a firm—for high-school and college students to spend a day or a week with a seasoned designer, tagging along on their daily tasks such as client meetings or visits to construction sites.

Students seek internships in several ways, including employment website platforms such as Handshake, professional organizations' job boards, firm websites, and interior design program connections (local firms often reach out to program heads or faculty when looking for strong interns). LinkedIn is also a popular platform to connect with professionals, possible employers, and other alumni. Wherever someone finds their internship, the opportunity to learn more about the profession through hands-on experience in a firm, while building a résumé and portfolio, is priceless.

See also Education, page 210

When one thinks about all the interior spaces that humans use every day, it's astounding how many spaces there are to design. While not all spaces are designed by a professional, the strongest ones are—and, since interiors don't have lasting power in the way that architecture does (spaces are outgrown or wear out, and that's fine), interior designers have a lot of opportunities to work, especially in cities and urban areas.

Interior designers work on different project types within a variety of companies and **firm types**. Size, organization, location, and expertise all factor into what makes one firm different from another. There are interior design firms, architecture firms with interior designers on staff, and in-house interior designers in all types of corporations (for example, financial, medical, hospitality, academic, retail). In-house designers often work in the facilities sector, where they design and manage spaces for a company. Another example is the in-house interior designer for a hotel brand. While the overall design and private rooms are done by the hotel, high-end ones may outsource public spaces such as the lobby or restaurants to a renowned designer with a signature style for increased visibility. In this case, the in-house designer manages the overall project® while serving as a mediator between the hired designer and the hotel.

Interior designers work in product and showroom sales; exhibit and production design; lighting consulting; and real estate (just to name a few). This book focuses on several project types, but any space that people use can be designed, and so designers touch all aspects of human life. Think about all the places encountered during one entire day, and how the interiors connect to each experience from beginning to end.

See also Hotels, page 100, and Restaurants, page 102

10.5 —— Profession

Designer   Think! Architecture and Design
Project   Think! Architecture and Design Office
Location   Brooklyn, NY, US

Once a graduate lands a full-time entry-level job, they can slowly work their way up through the hierarchy of **firm roles** through proven job success and experience. Firm titles range in name and scope; however, many designers start as a junior interior designer. More focused positions may have specific titles such as space planner, AutoCAD/Revit designer, or FF+E specialist. With hard work, companies offer the opportunity for growth and new challenges, so that junior designers can move on to *interior design assistant*; then *interior designer*; *project manager*; *senior interior designer*; *director*; and, finally, *associate*, *executive*, or *partner*. With each vertical move, or promotion, responsibilities increase, creating an incentive for motivated designers who want to keep challenging themselves (and a salary bump doesn't hurt either).

Small firms have less-structured roles, since their designers often work on all aspects of a job no matter where they fit in the hierarchy. Large firms are often organized into smaller "studios," which gives the feeling of working in a small to midsize firm, yet with larger projects and more resources. Designers with an entrepreneurial flair will seek to start their own firm, usually after working for someone else and gaining enough experience and confidence. Being the boss has its perks, especially when it comes to making the decisions, but it's also important that designers "know what they don't know," and hire employees and consultants who will balance their strengths and weaknesses.

It is also common for designers to move from firm to firm—especially within the first few years of their career—to try out different sizes and types of companies, since each experience can be vastly different. This is completely acceptable in the professional world, as the first 10 years of a designer's career are often looked at as extended education, mostly because there is so much to learn.

See also Coordination, page 204

Most interior design projects follow a similar **process**, no matter what the project type. Clients come with a set of needs and wants, and—most importantly—a budget. The designer conducts interviews to understand the priorities, and will balance them with the space and budget available. It's like a puzzle, trying to fit many components into set parameters while applying required codes so that spaces are functional, healthy, safe, aesthetically pleasing, and humanistic.

A key component for the initial design phase is research. For every project, there is always something to learn, which keeps the profession exciting after years of practice. The designer studies the context, which includes the history of the building for an existing structure or the drawings for a new building; the site, from macro (country or city) to micro (neighborhood); and the culture of the location. It is also important for the designer to understand the ethos of the client, brand, or company as well as new methodologies for the project type.

The designer then translates ideas into three-dimensional (physical) space. Freehand sketching allows creativity to flow naturally; many designers continue to sketch with pencil or pen and rolls of tracing paper, while others utilize digital technology such as an iPad and stylus. Within this programming phase, the designer explores spatial hierarchy and how the user will experience the space. They use tools such as bubble diagrams, adjacency matrices, and diagramming. Diagrams are clear, graphic drawings that emphasize ideas, break down complex ideas, and communicate design ideas to the client. What follows is the schematic design phase; that's when the interior really starts to evolve through orthographic drawings (floor plans, elevations, sections) and preliminary material selections that give a feel for the space.

See also Research, page 54, and Context, page 56

Designer   Design, Bitches
Project   Design, Bitches Office
Location   Los Angeles, CA, US

After the schematic design is complete, presented to the client, and approved, the designer moves on to the design development phase of the **process**. This incorporates further evolution of the drawings, as well as advanced material and furniture selection. This stage commences with a more robust presentation to the client, and approval signals the start of the construction drawings—a comprehensive set of documents given to the contractor and used to build the project.

The CD set, as it is often referred to, incorporates many plans, including a demolition plan (what is being demolished), a construction plan (new partitions, doors, and built-ins, with dimensions and finishing specifications), lighting plans (floor, wall, and ceiling lighting, including switching and dimming systems), and a reflected ceiling plan (beams, coffers, finishes, and location of mechanical ducts, vents, and sprinklers). Aside from the plans, there are elevations (two-dimensional drawings with dimensions and notes), sections (vertical cuts through the space), and details (large-scale drawings). CDs also have door, hardware, lighting, equipment, and finishing schedules, listing all the items to be ordered by the contractor.

With the CDs complete, the designer sends the set out to contractors for bidding and pricing (typically three bids for comparison). At some point, the CDs must also be approved by the governing jurisdiction for a permit. After the client selects the contractor, the contracts are signed, the permit is received…and the work begins! Designers are then involved in construction administration, which involves meeting regularly on-site with a variety of disciplines and trades. With construction underway, furniture, floor and wallcoverings, decorative lighting, and accessories are ordered through purchase orders from the interior designer, who provides follow-through and coordination for the final installation. In larger commercial projects, the materials and furniture are often purchased by the general contractor.

Through organization and collaboration, the project finally comes together. Let's just say that the old image of the interior design professional simply picking paint colors and selecting pillows could not be more outdated.

See also Construction Administration, page 202, and Coordination, page 204

Designer   Design, Bitches
Project   Design, Bitches Office
Location   Los Angeles, CA, US

The interior design profession has evolved from socialites decorating homes into a fully fledged profession of diverse, educated creatives designing residential, commercial, and institutional projects. In tandem with an organized payment method for services and expanding project types, **professional organizations** worked to formalize and validate interior design as a recognized discipline.

In the United States, there are two main professional organizations. The American Society of Interior Designers (ASID), which began in the mid-20th century as the American Institute of Decoration (AID), replaced the term "decoration" with "design," and in 1970 merged with a similar body to become ASID. The International Interior Design Association (IIDA), resulting from a merger of three design-related organizations, was established in 1994. Both ASID and IIDA offer connections within the interior design community through events, competitions, education, and more. The equivalent body in the UK is the British Institute of Interior Design (BIID).

With the discipline increasing in complexity, the Council for Interior Design Qualification (CIDQ) was developed in 1974 to provide a baseline examination for the profession, which assesses knowledge in topics such as human behavior, construction drawings, and building systems. In 1982, the first US legislation for professional licensure was passed so that there would be legal requirements for practice, which vary according to location. For example, several states require a person to be registered as a professional interior designer when working on unsupervised commercial spaces. While licensure is dependent on location, in the United States many interior designers take the National Council for Interior Design Qualification (or NCIDQ) exam as a professional goal, which communicates their "expertise in understanding and applying current codes established to protect public health, safety, and welfare," as stated on the CIDQ website.

See also Certification, page 164

Event   IIDA Industry Roundtable 23
Location   Los Angeles, CA, US

One thing is clear: the interior designer never stops learning. Through education, internship, full-time employment, and professional development, designers are constantly finding new inspiration on materials, products, and methods to create innovative interiors that push the field of creativity forward. Every client, project, or design problem is an opportunity to learn something new and make an impact on the users who experience the space.

That is why interior designers seek out professional development through **continuing education** programming. In the United States, licensed interior designers require continuing education units (CEUs) to maintain their certification credentials. One CEU equals 10 contact hours of a class or program, which is approved by interior design and architecture professional organizations. The Interior Design Continuing Education Council (IDCEC) is an organization that compiles offerings so that designers can search for topics of interest and organize their credits. Professional organizations host events that provide credits for those who participate, such as lectures and courses through webinars, in-person conferences, and trade shows. Council of Interior Design Accredication (CIDA)-accredited university courses are also approved as continuing education. In the UK, the British Institute of Interior Design requires its members to complete annual continuing professional development (CPD) requirements.

Another way in which designers can stay on top of trends and new developments is to attend design fairs and trade shows such as NeoCon in Chicago, the International Contemporary Furniture Fair (ICFF) in New York, and Salone del Mobile Milano. With products, lectures, galleries, and much more, these events provide endless inspiration. Passionate interior designers seek visual information, and there are many ways to access it, through books, periodicals, exhibits, retail experiences, films, documentaries, and more.

One thing is certain: design is *everywhere*!

See also Books, page 10, and Periodicals + Newspapers, page 12

Index

Index

Authors' Acknowledgments

Our deep gratitude goes to Liz Faber and the entire team at Laurence King for their guidance and unwavering support throughout the process, and to Violetta Boxill for her beautiful design. We also want to thank all the professional designers who happily shared their work, which so eloquently visualizes our thoughts about the interior design discipline. Finally, we want to acknowledge the GW Interior Architecture students whose creativity and hard work is shown in the Conceptual and Spatial chapters.

Picture Credits

11 Horst Friedrichs/Alamy Stock Photo **13** Courtesy of *Interior Design Magazine* © January 2021 **15** Laura Cattano **17** © AMC Networks, Inc. Photo: Justina Mintz/AMC **19** Courtesy Rockwell Group. Photo: Paul Warchol **21** Digital Image, the Museum of Modern Art, New York/Scala, Florence. Photo: Martin Beck **23** The Eli and Edythe L. Broad Collection © Estate of Roy Lichtenstein/DACS, 2024 **25 left** Diego Allen/Unsplash **25 right** Anton Oparin/Alamy Stock Photo **27** Minecraft Fins'n'Flippers © Mojang **29** Florence Knoll Bassett papers, 1932–2000. Archives of American Art, Smithsonian Institution. **33** Bates Masi + Architects **35–37** Yoshihiro Makino **39** Bruce Damonte **41** Jasper Sanidad **43** Sasha Bikoff **45** Pedro Pegenaute **47** Ema Peter **49** Clodagh **51** Bruce Damonte **55** Mary Armintrout **57** Magenta Livengood **59** Cece Witherspoon **61** Danielle Lee **63** sketch: Michelle Lin; notebook image: Katerina Sisperova/iStock **65** Magenta Livengood **67** Ryan Fowkes **69** Soorin Chung **71** Bryce Delaney **73** Stephanie Travis **77** Yeri Caceres **79** Anna Mackie **81** Abbie McGrann **82** Soorin Chung **85** Becca Friedman **87** Soorin Chung **89** Mengjiao Wang **91** Danielle Lee **93** Lindsay Sydness **95** Catherine Anderson **99** Laure Joliet **101–103** Wichmann + Bendtsen **105** Shen Zhonghai **107** © Robert Deitchler, courtesy of Gensler **109** Laure Joliet **111** Esto **113** Albert Vecerka/Esto **115** Christopher Payne/Esto **117** Jeff Goldberg/Esto **121** Ema Peter **123** Pedro Pegenaute **125** Space Copenhagen **127** Pedro Pegenaute **129** Runzi Zhu **131** Yoshiro Makino **133** Neri&Hu **135** Bates Masi + Architects **137** Maharam **139** Karim Rashid **143** Christian Horan Photography **145** Space Copenhagen **147** Joseph De Leo **149** Gordon Beall **151** Photo: Michael Biondo **153** Clodagh **155** Space Copenhagen **157–159** Laure Joliet **161** Sasha Bikoff **165** Photo © Aisling McCoy **167** Pedro Pegenaute **169** //3877 + KNEAD HD **171** Andy Stagg/VIEW **173** Lawrence Anderson/Esto **175** Seth Powers Photography **177** Bruce Damonte **179** Clodagh **181** Bates Masi + Architects **183** Pedro Pegenaute **187–197** //3877 + KNEAD HD **199** Material ConneXion **201–205** //3877 + KNEAD HD **209** Courtesy Royal College of Art ©RCA_SoA Facilities **211** Erdark/iStock **213** Sketches: Stephanie Travis; portfolio image: santol/iStock **215** Stock-Asso/Shutterstock **217** Christopher Payne/Esto **219** William Alfonso Arbizu **221–223** Misha Gravenor **225** Photo courtesy of IIDA and Greg Chappell **227** Hero Images/Alamy Stock Photo